TAKE A
HIKE

Family Walks in New York's
Finger Lakes Region

by Rich & Sue Freeman

Cover Design by Michael A. Lynch, www.bookcoverdesign.com
Maps by Rich Freeman
Pictures by Rich & Sue Freeman

Cover Picture by Andy Olenick, Fotowerks, Ltd., www.fotowerks.com

ISBN   978-1-930480-20-9
        1-930480-20-2

Manufactured in the United States of America

Library of Congress Control Number: 2006924003

Every effort has been made to provide accurate and up-to-date trail descriptions in this book. Hazards are noted where known, but conditions change constantly. Users of this book are reminded that they alone are responsible for their own safety when on any trail and that they use the routes described in this book at their own risk. Void where prohibited, taxed, or otherwise regulated. Contents may settle during shipping. Use only as directed. Discontinue use if a rash develops.

The authors, publishers, and distributors of this book assume no responsibility for any injury, misadventure, fine, arrest or loss occurring from use of the information contained herein.

If you find inaccurate information or substantially different conditions (after all, things do change), please send a note detailing your findings to:
    Footprint Press, Inc., 303 Pine Glen Court, Englewood, FL 34223
    or email: info@footprintpress.com

TAKE A
HIKE

Family Walks in New York's
Finger Lakes Region

Footprint Press Inc.

303 Pine Glen Court, Englewood, FL 34223
www.footprintpress.com

Footprint Press publishes a variety of outdoor recreation guidebooks. See a complete list and order form at the back of this book. We also publish a free, monthly ezine (electronic magazine) on outdoor recreation in central and western New York.
To sign up visit: www.footprintpress.com

Locations by Trail Number

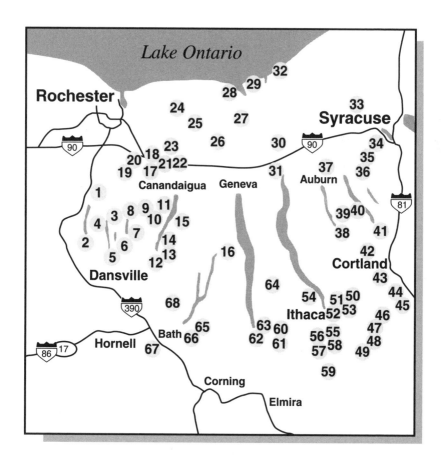

Contents

Acknowledgments

The research, writing, production, and promotion of a book such as this is never a solitary adventure. *Take A Hike* came into being because of the assistance of many wonderful people who freely shared their knowledge, experience, resources, thoughts, and time. We extend our heartfelt thanks to them all. Each in his or her own way is responsible for making the Finger Lakes Region a better place to live and, most of all, a community rich with the spirit of collaboration for the betterment of all. This is what ensures quality of life within a community. Thank you, each and every one.

People associated with the organizations listed as contacts for each trail directed us to choice trails, reviewed our maps and descriptions, supplied historical tidbits, and often are responsible for the existence and maintenance of the trails. Our heartfelt thanks extend to:

Autumn Greenberg, Cayuga Nature Center
Lois Kozlowski, Wizard of Clay Pottery
Rose Mary Luther, Town of Richmond, Sandy Bottom Nature Trail
Evelyn Gay Mills, Genesee Land Trust
Margarita Neumann, Olga Fleisher Ornithology Foundation, Inc.
Anne M. Reinhardt, The Nature Conservancy
W. Riddell, Town of Ontario Parks & Recreation Department
Irene Szabo, Finger Lakes Trail Conference
Dave Wright, Victor Hiking Trails
Andrew Zepp, Finger Lakes Land Trust

Introduction

"When the glaciers came they left in their wake a realm of gentle hills. And when the sun rose for the first time upon the new land, a spirit of the earth saw it and thought it so beautiful that he laid his hands upon the ground to bless it. When his hands were moved, the hollows left by his fingers were filled with water."

A local legend provided by the Finger Lakes Interpretive Center

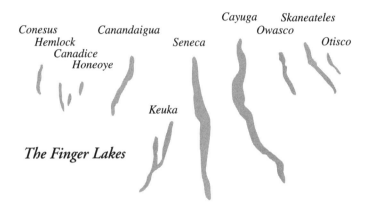

Conesus Canandaigua Cayuga Skaneateles
Hemlock Seneca Owasco Otisco
Canadice
Honeoye
Keuka

The Finger Lakes

Take a hike or a short walk. It's good for you. In as little as one hour you can do your body a favor – stretch your legs, raise your heart rate, and decrease your stress level. Hiking is a perfect exercise to balance today's hectic lifestyle.

Over the past years we have enjoyed hiking in many states throughout the United States. It didn't matter if it was a brief walk or an extended backpacking trip. Every time we ventured outside, Mother Nature offered something new and wonderful. We learned it's not necessary to go far to reap these benefits.

In 1997 we wrote and published *Take A Hike! Family Walks in the Rochester Area* which described 40 short hikes in Monroe and Ontario Counties. We were heartened by the reaction to that book. Families used it to expose their kids to the abundance of nature; people of all ages and abilities used it as part of an exercise program; and newcomers used it to learn about the area. As we continued hiking, we'd pass people on trails with our book clasped tightly in their hands. Generally the book looked tattered and well-worn. It always made us smile. People were using the resource we so lovingly provided.

We went on to produce 14 other guidebooks, including a previous edition to this guide that covered both the Finger Lakes Region and the Genesee Valley Region. Every year new trails were built, so for this edition we've pared the geography down to cover just the Finger Lakes Region - more trails in a smaller geographic area.

If you want even longer trails to hike, please check out *Take Your Bike! Family Rides in the Finger Lakes Region*. It's chock full of long trails that are great for hiking as well as bicycling.

Many of the trails in this book were built and are maintained by volunteer or community groups. They all welcome new members. We encourage everyone to join and benefit from the wide range of resources available in the Finger Lakes Region.

Most trails listed in this book are free and open to the public. A few require a small admission fee or request a donation. They are clearly noted in the heading to each trail beside the term "Admission." You do not have to be a member of the sponsoring group to enjoy any of the trails.

If you find inaccurate information or substantially different conditions (after all, things do change), please send a note detailing your findings to:

Footprint Press, 303 Pine Glen Court, Englewood, FL 34223
email: info@footprintpress.com

How To Use This Book

We have clustered the hikes into five groups using county boundaries as groupings except for Cayuga County:

Walks in Livingston, Ontario, & Yates Counties
Walks in Wayne, Seneca, & Cayuga Counties
Walks in Onondaga, Cayuga & Cortland Counties
Walks in Tompkins County
Walks in Schuyler & Steuben Counties

We selected the trails with variety in mind. Some of the better known trails are popular and heavily traveled, but their splendor made it hard for us to leave them out. Most of the trails are lesser known and lightly traveled. We also selected trails which are fairly easy to follow or well marked. Areas with many intersecting trails (where we got lost) were excluded.

Where possible, we have designated hikes that go in a loop to let you see as much as possible without backtracking. You can easily begin and end in one location and not worry about finding transportation back to the beginning.

Approximate hiking times are given, but of course this depends on your speed. If you stop to watch the wildlife, enjoy the views, or read the descriptive plaques, it will take you longer than the time given. You'll notice that many of the hikes also have shortcuts or are connected to other trails that allow you to adjust your time.

The maps for each trail are just sketches. We wanted maps that were easy to view and understand so everyone could be comfortable looking at where they were going and what they were seeing. Some of the sketches were taken from more detailed maps showing overall general location relative to intersecting trails and landscape features. Some areas were never mapped for hiking trails prior to this book.

Advances in technology have allowed us to improve upon all the maps, even ones that were included in the previous edition of this book. We were able to GPS track the trails to provide more accurate maps and to provide GPS coordinates for the parking area, making it easier to find the trails.

Legend

At the beginning of each trail listing, you will find a map and description with the following information:

Location: The closest town or lake and the county the trail is in.

Directions: How to find the trailhead parking area from a major road or town.

Alternative Parking: Other parking locations with access to the trail. Use these if you want to shorten your hike by starting or stopping at a spot other than the designated end point.

Hiking Time: Approximate time to hike at a comfortable pace (about 2 miles per hour), including time to enjoy the views.

Length: The round-trip length of the hike in miles (unless noted as one-way).

Difficulty:

(1 boot) easy hiking, generally level trail

(2 boots) rolling hills, gradual grades on trail

(3 boots) gentle climbing required to follow the trail

(4 boots) some strenuous climbing required

Surface: The materials that make up the trail surface for the major portion of the hike.

Trail Markings: Markings used to designate the trails in this book vary widely. Some trails are not marked at all but can be followed by cleared or worn paths. This doesn't pose a problem for the hiker as long as there aren't many intersecting, unmarked paths. Other trails are well marked with either signs, blazes, or markers, and sometimes a combination of all three. Blazing is done by the official group that maintains the trail.

Signs – wooden or metal signs with instructions in words or pictures.

Blazes – painted markings on trees showing where the trail goes. Many blazes are rectangular and placed at eye level. (See the picture on page 274.) Colors may be used to denote different trails. If a tree has twin blazes beside one another, you should proceed cautiously because the trail either turns or another trail intersects.

Sometimes you'll see a section of trees with painted markings which aren't neat geometric shapes. These are probably boundary markers or trees marked for logging. Trail blazes are generally distinct geometric shapes and are placed at eye level.

Markers – small plastic or metal geometric shapes (square, round, triangular) nailed to trees at eye level to show where the trail goes. They also may be colored to denote different trails.

It is likely that at some point you will lose the blazes or markers while following a trail. The first thing to do is stop and look around. See if you can spot a blaze or marker by looking in all directions, including behind you. If not, backtrack until you see a blaze or marker, then proceed forward again, carefully following the markings.

Uses: Each trail has a series of icons depicting the activity or activities allowed on the trail. Jogging is allowed on all trails, as is snowshoeing when snow covers the ground. The icons include:

Hiking

Bicycling

Cross-country
Skiing

Wheelchairs

Horseback
Riding

Snow-
mobiling

Admission: This line will only appear if there is an admission charge to use the trails. In that case, it will state how much is recommended for the fee or donation.

Contact: The address and phone number of the organization to contact if you would like additional information or if you have questions not answered in this book.

13

Map Legend

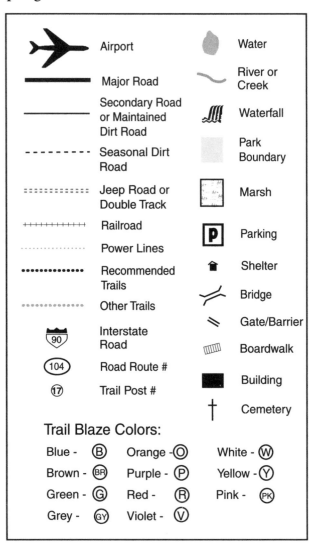

✈	Airport	Water	
▬▬▬▬	Major Road	River or Creek	
————	Secondary Road or Maintained Dirt Road	Waterfall	
- - - - - -	Seasonal Dirt Road	Park Boundary	
=====	Jeep Road or Double Track	Marsh	
+++++++	Railroad	Parking	
··········	Power Lines	Shelter	
●●●●●●	Recommended Trails	Bridge	
○○○○○○	Other Trails	Gate/Barrier	
90	Interstate Road	Boardwalk	
104	Road Route #	Building	
17	Trail Post #	Cemetery	

Trail Blaze Colors:

Blue - Ⓑ	Orange - Ⓞ	White - Ⓦ
Brown - ⒝ⓡ	Purple - Ⓟ	Yellow - Ⓨ
Green - Ⓖ	Red - Ⓡ	Pink - ⓟⓚ
Grey - ⒢ⓨ	Violet - Ⓥ	

Directions

In the directions we often tell you to turn left or right. To avoid confusion, in some instances we have noted a compass direction in parentheses according to the following:

(N)	= north	(S)	= south
(E)	= east	(W)	= west

Some trails have "Y" or "T" junctions. A "Y" junction indicates one path that turns into two paths. The direction we give is either bear left or bear right. A "T" junction is one path that ends at another. The direction is turn left or turn right.

Guidelines

Any adventure in the outdoors can be inherently dangerous. It's important to watch where you are going and keep an eye on children. Some of these trails are on private property where permission is benevolently granted by the landowners. Please respect the landowners and their property. Follow all regulations posted on signs and stay on the trails. Our behavior today will determine how many of these wonderful trails remain for future generations to enjoy.

Follow "no-trace" ethics whenever you venture outdoors. "No-trace" ethics means that the only thing left behind as evidence of your passing is your footprints. Carry out all trash you carry in. Do not litter. In fact, carry a plastic bag with you and pick up any litter you happen upon along the way. The trails included in this book are intended for day hikes. Please, no camping or fires.

As the trails age and paths become worn, trail work groups sometimes reroute the trails. This helps control erosion and allows vegetation to return. It also means that if a sign or marker doesn't appear as it is described in the book, it's probably due to trail improvement.

Remember:

Take only pictures, leave only footprints.

Please do not pick anything.

Preparations and Safety

You can enhance your time in the outdoors by dressing properly and carrying appropriate equipment. Even for a short day hike, take a small backpack or fanny pack with the following gear:

camera	flashlight
binoculars	insect spray or lotion
compass	water bottle with water
rain gear	nature guidebook(s) of flowers, birds, etc.
snacks	plastic bag to pick up trash

Many of the trails can be muddy. It's best to wear lightweight hiking boots or at least sturdy sneakers.

Walking sticks have been around for centuries, but they are finding new life and new forms in recent years. These sticks can be anything from a branch picked up along the trail to a $200 pair of poles designed with built-in springs and hand-molded grips. Using a walking stick is a good idea, especially in hilly terrain. It can take the pressure off your knees and help you balance when crossing bridges or logs. Two hiking poles (one for each hand) are even better.

Hiking with children is good exercise as well as an opportunity for learning. Use the time to teach children how to read a compass, identify flowers, trees, birds, and animal tracks. You'll find books on each of these subjects in the public library.

Make it fun by taking a different type of gorp for each hike. Gorp originated as an acronym for **G**ood **O**ld **R**aisins and **P**eanuts. Today, Gorp is any combination of dried foods that you eat as a snack. Examples are:

1) peanuts, M&Ms®, and raisins
2) chocolate morsels, nuts, and granola
3) dried banana chips, sunflower seeds, and carob chips

Get creative and mix any combination of chocolate, carob, dried fruits, nuts, oats, granolas, etc. The bulk food section at your local grocery store has a wealth of ideas. Other fun snacks are marshmallows, popcorn, peanuts in shells, graham crackers, and beef jerky.

When hiking with a child, tie a string on a whistle and have your child wear it as a necklace for safety. Instruct your child to blow the whistle only if he or she is lost.

Dogs Welcome!

Hiking with dogs can be fun because of their keen sense of smell and different perspective on the world. Many times they find things that we would have passed. They're inquisitive about everything and make excellent companions. To ensure that you and your hiking companion enjoy the time outside, you must control your dog. Dogs are required to be leashed on most maintained public trails. The reasons are numerous, but the main ones are to protect dogs, to protect other hikers, and to ensure that your pet doesn't chase wildlife. Good dog manners go a long way toward creating goodwill and improving tolerance toward their presence.

59 of the trails listed in this book welcome dogs. Please respect the requirement that dogs be leashed where noted.

The only trails which **prohibit dogs** are:

Trail #	Trail Name
8	Sandy Bottom Nature Trail
11	Onanda Park
22	MaryFrances Bluebird Haven
27	Huckleberry Swamp
33	Beaver Lake Nature Center
34	Camillus Forest Unique Area
36	Baltimore Woods
51	Sapsucker Woods
54	Cayuga Nature Center

Seasons

Most people head into the great outdoors in summer. Temperatures are warm, the days are long, and plants and wildlife are plentiful. Summer is a great time to go hiking. However, don't neglect the other seasons.

Each season offers a unique perspective, and makes hiking the same trail a totally different adventure. In spring, a time of rebirth, you can watch the leaves unfurl and the spring flowers burst.

Become a leaf peeper in fall. Venture forth onto the trails and take in the colorful splendor of a beautiful fall day. Listen to the rustle of newly fallen leaves under your feet and inhale the unique smell of this glorious season.

The only complication with fall is that it coincides with the hunting season. Many of the trails in this guide book are on public lands where hunting is permitted. When hiking in the fall, be sure to wear bright colors (preferably blaze orange) and if possible select hiking locations that are not on hunting grounds. The hunting season around the Finger Lakes Region is generally:

> Archery hunting: mid-October to mid-December
> Shotgun hunting: mid-November to mid-December

And, finally, winter. It may be cold out, but the leaves are off the trees and the views will never be better. You can more fully appreciate the variety of this area's terrain if you wander out in winter. It is also the perfect time to watch for animal tracks in the snow and test your identification skills.

Land Types

The walks detailed in this book traverse a variety of public and private lands. Regardless of ownership, the land deserves our respect and care. Please tread lightly, stay on the trails, obey posted regulations, and carry out everything you carried in.

The New York State Department of Conservation (DEC) and the National Forest Service employ foresters and biologists to oversee lands managed for various purposes. A century ago, only 26% of New York State was covered by forest. Today, 62% is forested.

National and State Forests: Since 1929, when New York State began purchasing and reforesting abandoned farmland, foresters have changed this once-depleted land into the finest forests in the state. The 700,000 acres of state forests and multiple use areas give New Yorkers improved water quality, a sustainable wood supply, and the opportunity for a wide variety of outdoor recreational experiences. Foresters also manage these lands to provide a diversity of wildlife habitats and to protect and enhance populations of rare and endangered species.

Unique Areas: DEC purchases unique areas to preserve unusual ecosystems. An example is the Camillus Unique Area where a nearly old growth forest is being saved for posterity.

Wildlife Management Areas and Wildlife Refuges: These areas are dedicated to perpetuating wildlife species, demonstrating management practices, and providing wildlife-related recreational activities. Wildlife biologists and foresters work together to manage the 175,000 acres that make up the State's Wildlife Management Areas.

Many other lands are opened to hikers through the hard work and generous spirit of government agencies, conservation and nature societies, and a myriad of volunteers.

State, County, Town, and City Parks: These lands are generally developed for public recreational uses. They often have nature or interpretive centers, shelters or pavilions, restrooms, picnic facilities, and other amenities.

Nature Preserves and Nature Centers: These privately owned lands are often open for public use. They are managed by organizations such as nature conservancies, land trusts, Aububon Societies, and museums.

Organizations: The Finger Lakes Region is blessed with having volunteer organizations that either purchase lands to develop trail systems or work with private landowners to obtain permission for trails to cross private lands. These include organizations such as Ontario Pathways, Victor Hiking Trails, Cayuga Trails Club, Friends of the Finger Lakes Outlet, Friends of Blue Cut, Finger Lakes Trail Conference and the Finger Lakes Land Trust.

Finger Lakes Trail
and Connecting Trails

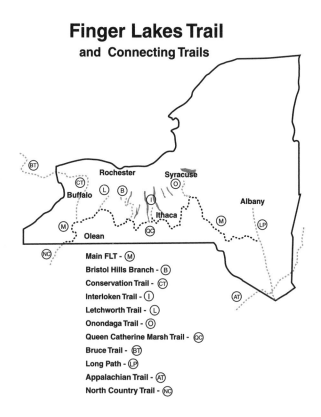

Main FLT - Ⓜ
Bristol Hills Branch - Ⓑ
Conservation Trail - ⓒⓣ
Interloken Trail - Ⓘ
Letchworth Trail - Ⓛ
Onondaga Trail - Ⓞ
Queen Catherine Marsh Trail - ⓠⓒ
Bruce Trail - ⓑⓣ
Long Path - ⓛⓟ
Appalachian Trail - ⓐⓣ
North Country Trail - ⓝⓒ

The Finger Lakes Trail

The Finger Lakes Trail Conference is unique in the scope of its endeavors within the area. The Finger Lakes Trail stretches for 559 miles from Allegheny State Park in southwestern New York State, across the bottom of the Finger Lakes, into the Catskill Mountains north of New York City. Part of it is also the North Country National Scenic Trail which will eventually span from North Dakota to eastern New York State. The Finger Lakes Trail connects with the Long Path which connects with the Appalachian Trail. At the western end, by way of the Conservation Trail it connects to the Bruce Trail. The Finger Lakes Trail has six branch trails totalling 238 miles, creating an extensive trail network.

Thirteen trails in this guide utilize segments of the Finger Lakes Trail. They are:

Trail #	Trail Name
#12	Hi Tor Wildlife Management Area
#44	James B. Kennedy State Forest - Virgil Mountain Loop
#45	Tuller Hill State Forest
#46	Spanish & Irvin Loop Trails
#49	Shindagin Hollow State Forest
#56	Sweedler Preserve
#59	Abbott Loop in Danby State Forest
#60	Bob Cameron Loop Trail
#61	Van Lone Hill Loop Trail
#63	Texas Hollow State Forest
#64	Finger Lakes National Forest
#65	Birdseye Hollow State Forest
#68	Urbana State Forest

All 800 plus miles of the Finger Lakes Trail System and its campsites are open to the public for hiking adventures. The trail system is built and maintained entirely by volunteers with financial support from membership dues and map and guidebook sales. The Finger Lakes Trail Conference recently revised all their maps using GPS information and printed them in full color. Contact them for a map buyer's guide and membership information: Finger Lakes Trail Conference

6111 Visitor Center Road, Mt. Morris, N.Y. 14510
(585) 658-9320
www.fingerlakestrail.org.

Finger Lakes Land Trust

Another non-profit organization in the Finger Lakes Region that leaves us awestruck by their accomplishments is the Finger Lakes Land Trust.

They establish nature preserves, hold conservation easements, educate the public for responsible stewardship, and work cooperatively with private groups and public agencies. Through a variety of means, they have provided protection for thousands of acres of wetlands, streams, meadows, forests, farmlands and shrublands throughout the Finger Lakes Region. These lands are rich with a diversity of wildlife and plants.

Finger Lakes Land Trust properties included in this guidebook are:

Trail #	Trail Name
# 7	Wesley Hill Nature Preserve
#14	Nundawao — The Great Hill Preserve
#40	Bahar Nature Preserve
#41	High Vista Nature Preserve
#42	Dorothy McIlroy Bird Sanctuary
#48	Goetchius Wetland Preserve
#50	Etna Nature Preserve
#52	Ellis Hollow Nature Preserve
#56	Sweedler Preserve
#57	Lindsay-Parsons Biodiversity Preserve
#66	Parker Nature Preserve

The Finger Lakes Land Trust is supported by donations from members and grants received from private foundations and government agencies. Over 200 active volunteers work hard to achieve land protection. Please consider joining this organization to offer your skills, talents and enthusiasm to continue this noble cause. Or, make a monetary contribution. Funds are always needed to improve signage and build boardwalks, bridges and kiosks at the nature preserves.

Finger Lakes Land Trust
202 East Court Street, Ithaca, NY 14850
(607) 275-9487   www.fllt.org

Walks in Livingston, Ontario and Yates Counties

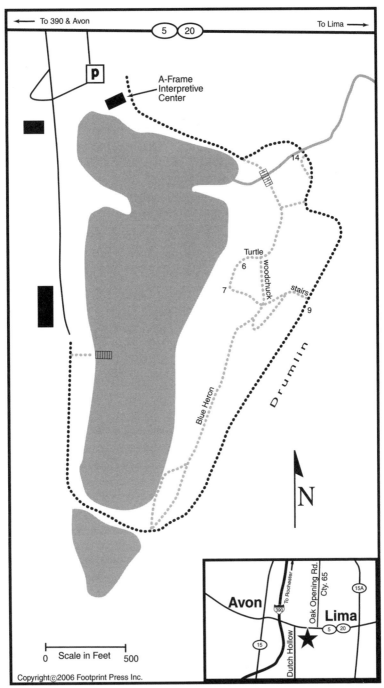

Twin Cedars Environmental Area

1.

Twin Cedars Environmental Area

Location:	East Avon, Livingston County
Directions:	On the south side of Route 5 & 20, east of Route 390. Pull into DEC Region 8 Headquarters. Bear left and park in front of the red A-frame building (obscured by tall arborvitaes). N42° 54.175 - W77° 40.149
Hiking Time:	35-minute loop
Length:	1.0-mile loop on Drumlin Trail (darkened) 1.6 miles of total trails
Difficulty:	👟 👟 👟
Surface:	Dirt and mowed-grass trails
Trail Markings:	Brown and yellow trail name signs at some trail intersections
Uses:	🚶 🎿
Dogs:	OK on leash
Contact:	N.Y.S. Department of Environmental Conservation 6274 East Avon-Lima Road, Avon, NY 14414 (585) 226-2466 www.dec.state.ny.us

Twin Cedars Environmental Area began in 1970 when the DEC purchased farmland adjacent to its offices. In 1974, the DEC purchased another 59 acres and enlarged the pond. In the 1980s the area was developed into an educational area, designed to emphasize the natural and man-made aspects of environmental conservation.

The A-frame building serves as an interpretive center. It is loaded with taxidermied animals, an extensive collection of bird eggs, along with live fish and turtles. The exhibits and displays are designed to test visitors' environmental knowledge and stimulate their curiosity. It is open year-round, most weekdays from 8:00 AM until 4:30 PM. Call ahead to make sure the interpretive center is open to the public on the day of your visit. The trails are open all the time.

The pond has been stocked with largemouth bass, black crappie, bluegills, pumpkinseeds, and tiger muskies. In 1993, triploid grass carp were added as a biological agent to control aquatic vegetation. Fishing is

A Canada goose enjoys the Twin Cedars pond.

permitted with a valid license. Any triploid grass carp caught must be returned to the pond.

Hike any loop you prefer. The outer perimeter is 1.2 miles in length. It circumnavigates the pond and takes you along the top of a high drumlin, or glacially-formed hill. The trails have numbered signs along the way. The numbers correspond to the trail guide listed below and help you understand the conservation practices in this environmental area.

Interpretive numbered signs:

#1. Birds can benefit from man-made nesting structures. As you walk the trail, notice the purple martin condos, bluebird houses, wood duck boxes, nesting rafts for geese, and nesting tripods for mallards.

#2. The dike on which you are standing was built to impound naturally flowing water, creating this pond. The pond provides a suitable habitat for many amphibians, reptiles, birds, mammals, and fish that would not otherwise live here.

#3. This wet area is known as a seep spring, and some of the plants here are unique to this spot. Stepping off the trail could damage this fragile ecosystem.

#4. A clue to unseen moisture, the horsetail is the last surviving member of an ancient group of plants that once grew 40 feet tall.

#5. The pond shallows are rich in aquatic life because sunlight reaches all the way to the bottom. Look for a variety of plants, insects, reptiles, fish, birds, and mammals.

#6. Many of the trees and shrubs here were planted to provide food and cover for wildlife. Can you identify autumn olive, silky dogwood, highbush cranberry, and staghorn sumac?

#7. An area containing only one species of plant is called a monoculture. Notice how these white pines have been planted in rows. These "plantations" can be an effective way to raise timber, but lack the diversity to attract much wildlife. Although it provides shelter to some species, its food value is limited.

#8. This white oak provides a haven for many seedlings under its canopy. Notice the small oaks in the area that originated from this tree. Ground plants compete with the young oaks, so only the strongest survive.

Walking a wide, mowed path at Twin Cedars.

#9. Poison ivy! All parts of this plant are poisonous. It grows as a ground cover, an erect shrub, or a climbing vine. The white berries are eaten by 60 species of birds, but people who touch poison ivy run the risk of forming itchy blisters.

#10. This land was once covered by a glacier one mile thick. As the glacier retreated 15,000 to 20,000 years ago, rock and soil were deposited, forming the hill or drumlin you are standing on.

#11. The tall grass in front of you is switchgrass. It was planted to provide cover for pheasants. Pheasants need tall grass for nesting in spring and hiding from predators the rest of the year.

#12. The area to the left is mowed periodically to keep it in grass. The border between different cover types (water, grass, woods, etc.) is called "edge." Many animals are attracted to edges because they provide more food and shelter than a single cover type.

#13. Notice that several white cedar trees have fallen over. That's because a nearby spring makes water readily available near the surface so the roots do not need to be deep. As the tree gets older, a strong wind can blow it over.

#14. This shallow brook has an ecosystem quite different from the pond. What makes it different? What types of plants and animals in the pond would not be found in the stream?

Trail Directions

• From the parking area, walk south past the A-frame building, toward the pond.

• Bear left, walking on the mowed-grass dike along the pond.

• At the first junction, a left will take you up the drumlin. (A right will keep you lower on the hill.)

• Continue with the loop, bearing left at each trail junction, until you reach the paved DEC access road.

• Follow the access road back to the parking area.

Date Hiked: _____

Notes:

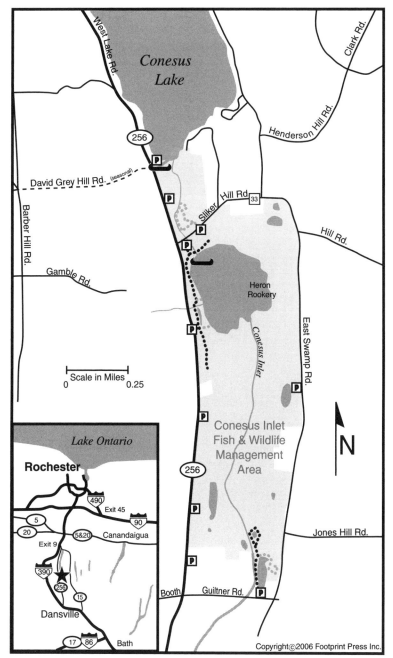

Conesus Inlet Trail

2.

Conesus Inlet Trail

Location: At the southern end of Conesus Lake, Livingston
                   County

Directions: From Interstate 390 use exit 9 (Route 15). Head south
                   on Route 256, then turn east on Sliker Hill Road. The
                   parking area is on the south side of Sliker Hill Road,
                   near the corner of Route 256.

N42° 42.916 - W77° 42.738

Alternative Parking: Parking area on the north side of Sliker Hill Road.

Alternative Parking: Parking area farther south on Route 256.

N42° 42.450 - W77° 42.686

Alternative Parking: Parking area on Guiltner Road.

N42° 40.993 - W77° 42.192

Hiking Time: 1 hour round trip

Length: 2 miles round trip (northern darkened trail)

                   1 mile loop (southern darkened trail)

                   3.4 miles of trails total

Difficulty: 👣

Surface: 10-foot wide mowed-grass path

Trail Markings: 2.5-inch round, plastic DEC trail markers

Uses: 🚶 🎿

Dogs: OK on leash

Contact: N.Y.S. Department of Environmental Conservation

                   6274 East Avon-Lima Road, Avon, NY 14414

                   (585) 226-2466   www.dec.state.ny.us

The Conesus Inlet Fish and Wildlife Management Area occupies over
1,120 acres of wetland in a valley floodplain at the south end of Conesus
Lake. In the late 1960s, the New York State Department of Environmental
Conservation (DEC) purchased this land and initiated wildlife management programs to preserve and protect the vital wetland resource. An
additional 83 acres were purchased in 1979 to provide access to Conesus
Lake and to preserve a critical northern pike spawning habitat.

The main walk heads south from Sliker Hill Road, through woods along
the wetland area. Bring a lunch and enjoy a picnic along the way. The

DEC built a series of viewing platforms from which you're likely to see Canada geese, great blue herons, pheasants, ruffed grouse, and many other birds. Along the trail you'll also find evidence of muskrat, mink, raccoon, fox, and deer, which are abundant in the area. In early spring many people enjoy a walk to the end of the dike to watch walleye and carp spawn upstream.

Trail Directions

- From the parking area on the south side of Sliker Hill Road, follow the wood-lined gravel path then bear left onto an earthen dam. The trail dead-ends, but this is a good viewing area.
- Backtrack, but this time turn left to head south.
- The mowed paths lead to the southern parking area and farther to a dead end.

Date Hiked: _____

Notes:

For an additional little hike, cross Sliker Hill Road. This trail is 2 short loops (0.85 mile total) on a raised earthen berm through a marshy grassland area which is a pike spawning bed. The round trip will take about 20 minutes.

Date Hiked: _____

Notes:

The third option is to head south on Route 256, then turn east onto Guiltner Road. The parking area is just after the Conesus Inlet crossing on the left. This is a pretty hike along a pond with large dead trees. It ends in two loops, the northern one around a pond (a 1-mile walk) and the southeast one is a walk around the perimeter of a mowed field (a 1.5-mile walk). This area is sporadically maintained so it's best to go in early spring before the vegetation grows high.

Date Hiked: _____

Notes:

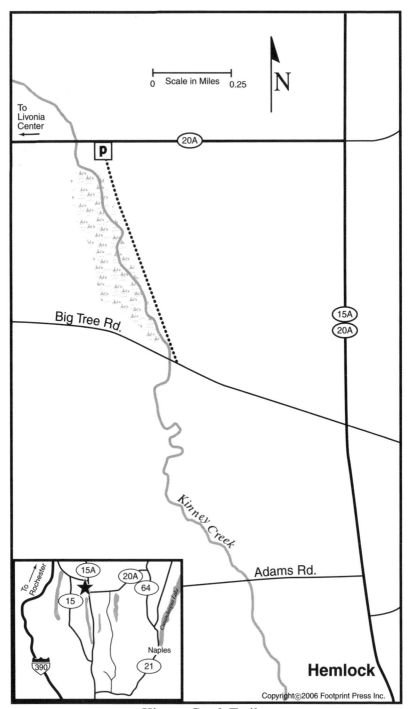

Kinney Creek Trail

3.

Kinney Creek Trail

Location:	Route 20A, Livonia Center, Livingston County
Directions:	From Route 15A, head west on Route 20A for 0.8 mile. Turn left at a bright blue metal building (7074 Route 20A, Livonia Highway Barns) and park on the left side in front of the chain-link fence. N42° 49.278 - W77° 37.666
Hiking Time:	45 minutes
Length:	1.5-mile round trip
Difficulty:	
Surface:	Dirt trail
Trail Markings:	None
Uses:	🚶 🎿 🚲
Dogs:	OK on leash
Contact:	Town of Livonia 36 Commercial Street, Livonia, NY 14487 (585) 346-3100

Built in 1998, this former railroad bed is now a narrow 0.75-mile long trail through trees and brush. Perfect for a quick escape into the woods.

Trail Directions
- Pass through the gate labeled "Enter here for Kinney Creek Trail" and head straight back.
- Follow the trail to Big Tree Road then turn around and walk back to Route 20A.

  Date Hiked: _____

  Notes:

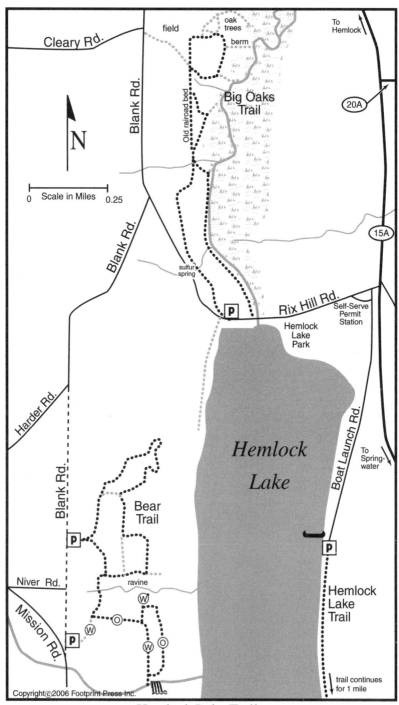

Hemlock Lake Trails
(Hemlock Lake Trail, Big Oaks Trail, Bear Trail)

4.

Hemlock Lake Trails
(Hemlock Lake Trail, Big Oaks Trail & Bear Trail)

Location:	The north end of Hemlock Lake, Livingston & Ontario Counties
Dogs:	OK on leash
Admission:	Free, but pick up a permit
Contact:	City of Rochester, Water and Lighting Bureau 7412 Rix Hill Road, Hemlock, NY 14466 (585) 428-3646

Long ago, Hemlock Lake had cottages all along its shore. In 1872 the city of Rochester decided to use Canadice and Hemlock Lakes as a water supply. The first conduit for water was completed in 1876. By 1947 Rochester had purchased all of the shoreline property and removed the cottages in order to help protect the water supply for its growing population. Although it was very difficult for the cottage residents to leave their land, this area is now free of the commercialization that is so rampant on the other Finger Lakes. Flow from Canadice Outlet Creek is diverted into the northern end of Hemlock Lake. From there the City of Rochester Water Bureau conditions the water for drinking and uses gravity to send it north for 29 miles via large pipes at a rate of up to 48 million gallons per 24-hour period.

Early settlers tried to farm around Hemlock Lake but found the glacially scoured land ill-suited for farming. Many areas around the lake were too steep or too wet for growing crops.

Today, the Hemlock and Canadice Lakes watershed continues to be Rochester's primary source of drinking water. The watershed covers more than 40,000 acres of land, of which Rochester owns 7,000 acres. A second-growth forest now prospers on the once forested land, and many abandoned farm fields have been reforested with conifers. Bald eagles are now present in the area.

To protect city property and the supply of drinking water, the city asks that all visitors obtain a Watershed Visitor Permit, one of the easiest permits to obtain. Just stop at the visitor's self-serve permit station located at the north end of Hemlock Lake on Rix Hill Road off

Route 15A (see the map on page 34) or download it at www.city-ofrochester.gov/watershedpermit.htm. There are no fees or forms to fill out, but the permit document details the dos and don'ts to help keep the area pristine, so it's important to read it. Swimming and camping are not permitted. Boats up to 16 feet long with motors up to 10 horsepower are okay. If you care to fish, the lake has salmon, trout, and panfish.

At the north end of Hemlock Lake, off Rix Hill Road, is beautiful Hemlock Lake Park, which has restrooms (May through mid-October), a pavilion with grills, and even a gazebo.

The exceptionally well-managed watershed area contains a variety of trees, including hemlock, beech, oak, maple, hickory, basswood, and white, red and scotch pine. You may see kingfishers, herons, ospreys, as well as bald eagles near the water. The relatively undisturbed forest along the trails is ideal habitat for several woodpecker species. Also, the narrow lake and forested shoreline create excellent sighting opportunities for spring and autumn migrating warblers and other songbirds.

Hemlock Lake Trail

Directions: From Route 15A at the north end of Hemlock Lake, turn west onto Rix Hill Road. Take the first left into the loop and pick up a permit at the self-serve permit area. From the loop, head south on Boat Launch Road to park at the end (near the boat launch).
N42º 45.8344 - W77º 36.6571

Alternative Parking: Park at the self-serve permit station and walk the dirt road (1.1 miles) to the boat launch.

Hiking Time: 2 hours round trip

Length: 3.6 miles round trip (from the boat launch)

Difficulty:

Surface: Double-track dirt and woodland trails

Trail Markings: None

Uses:

Facilities: Porta-Potty at boat launch

Walk a double-track dirt trail, packed hard from City of Rochester, Water and Lighting Bureau truck tires to a stone bench with a panoramic view of Hemlock Lake.

Trail Directions
- From the boat launch walk south past the grey metal gate.
- When the double-track ends (in 1.7 miles), cross the culvert and continue south on a narrow path through the woods.
- In another 0.1 mile you'll reach a stone bench overlooking Hemlock Lake, the perfect place for a contemplative break, and end of the trail.

Date Hiked: _____

Notes:

Big Oaks Trail

Directions:	From Route 15A at the north end of Hemlock Lake, turn west onto Rix Hill Road. Take the first left into the loop and pick up a permit at the self-serve permit area. Continue west on Rix Hill Road, cross Hemlock Lake Outlet and park at the trailhead on the right. N42º 46.669 - W77º 37.087
Hiking Time:	2 hour loop
Length:	3.2-mile loop
Difficulty:	🥾🥾🥾🥾
Surface:	Mowed-grass trails (may be tall grass, may be wet)
Trail Markings:	None
Uses:	

These trails head into a marshy area surrounding Hemlock Lake Outlet. They can be very wet in spring. However, it's a good place to look for spring and summer wildflowers. A portion of the trail follows the former bed of the Lehigh Valley Railroad. Watch for an old foundation near the sulfur spring.

Trail Directions
- Follow the grass trail (sporadically mowed) north.
- Cross two small streams.
- Continue straight on the old railroad grade.
- Stay right at the field to loop to the right then return south on the railroad bed.

• If you can find them, follow the two loops on the right. Depending on water conditions and the DEC mowing schedule, trails may appear different from what's shown on the map.

Date Hiked: _____

Notes:

Bear Trail

Directions:	From Route 15A at the north end of Hemlock Lake, turn west onto Rix Hill Road. Take the first left into the loop and pick up a permit at the self-serve permit area. Continue west on Rix Hill Road. Turn left (S) onto Blank Road. Pass Harder Road, then watch left for a parking area marked with an orange "Posted and Patrolled" sign. N42° 45.967 - W77° 37.867
Alternate Parking:	A dirt parking area on Blank Road between Niver and Mission Roads. N42° 45.641 - W77° 37.780
Hiking Time:	2-hour loop
Length:	3.5-mile loop (darkened trail)
	The flat trail between parking areas is 0.6-mile long.
	3.8 miles total trails
Difficulty:	👣 👣 👣 👣
Surface:	Mowed-grass trails through woods
Trail Markings:	Some colored markers
Uses:	🚶 🎿

The trails near Blank Road are flat but the other trails head downhill toward the lake with steep climbs in and out of gullies. This is a beautiful, pristine woods walk.

Bears are making a comeback in the Finger Lakes Region. In the early 1900s they were nearly hunted to extinction. By 2005 the census for the state estimated the population at about 7,000 bears, including approximately 400 that roam the Finger Lakes and Southern Tier Region. Experts say black bears are seldom dangerous, unless they're cornered or seeking food. Even a female with cubs is more likely to scurry up a tree to flee from a human threat (you). Count yourself lucky if you ever see a bear in the wild. You're most likely to only see its furry butt as it runs away.

Trail Directions
- From the northern parking area, follow the mowed grass path.
- Keep bearing left at every trail junction.
- If the trail dead ends, just turn around. One of the dead ends will supply a pretty waterfall. N42º 45.485 - W77º 37.493
- Toward the end, the white and orange blazes will help orient you and keep you from ending up at the southern parking lot.

Date Hiked: _____

Notes:

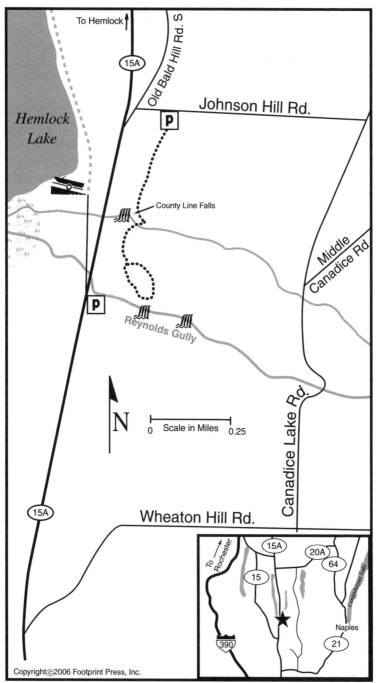

Johnson Hill Trail

5.

Johnson Hill Trail

Location:	Hemlock Lake, Livingston County
Directions:	From Route 15A at the south end of Hemlock Lake, turn east on Old Bald Hill Road South, then quickly turn right on Johnson Hill Road. In 0.1 mile turn right into a grassy parking area marked by a green and white "Hemlock-Canadice Watershed" hiker sign. N42º 40.580 - W77º 35.230
Hiking Time:	45 minute loop
Length:	1.5-mile loop
Difficulty:	👟👟👟👟
Surface:	Tall grass, sporadically mowed
Trail Markings:	None
Uses:	🚶 🎿
Dogs:	OK
Admission:	Free, but a Watershed Visitor Permit is required. Pick one up at the permit station on Rix Hill Road at the north end of Hemlock Lake or get it online at www.ci.rochester.ny.us/watershedpermit.htm
Contact:	City of Rochester, Water & Lighting Bureau 7412 Rix Hill Road, Hemlock, NY 14466 (585) 346-2617

Hemlock Lake is the drinking water supply for Rochester. To protect Rochester property and the supply of drinking water, the city requires all visitors to obtain a Watershed Visitor Permit, one of the easiest permits to obtain. Just stop at the visitor's self-serve, permit station located at the north end of Hemlock Lake on Rix Hill Road off Route 15A (see map on page 34) or go online to www.ci.rochester.ny.us/watershedpermit.htm. There are no fees or forms to fill out, but the permit details the do's and don'ts to help keep the area pristine, so it's important to read it.

Johnson Hill Trail will lead you past 50-foot-high County Line Falls in a drainage tributary to Hemlock Lake. The trail is generally unmowed, tall grass. It was developed in 1995 as part of a small timber harvest. In winter this trail makes a nice snowshoe route. At the far end of the loop you're at

41

County Line Falls tumbles toward Hemlock Lake.

the top of Reynolds Gully, but too high up to see any of its waterfalls. To explore additional waterfalls in the area, pick up a copy of *200 Waterfalls in Central and Western New York - A Finder's Guide* at www.footprintpress.com.

Trail Directions:
- From the parking area, hike past the metal gate on the wide, grass trail.
- Cross the creek (waterfall to the right) and bend right, heading uphill.
- Follow the loop at the end of the trail in either direction, then retrace your steps back to the parking area.

Date Hiked: _____

Notes:

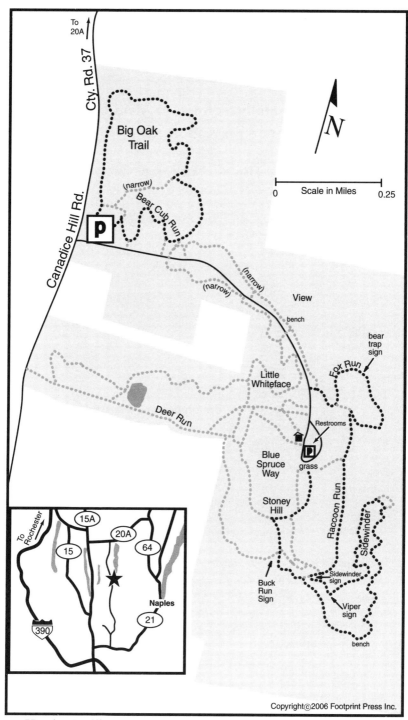

Harriet Hollister Spencer Memorial State Recreation Area

6.

Harriet Hollister Spencer Memorial
State Recreation Area

Location: South of Honeoye Lake, Ontario County
Directions: From Route 390, head east on Route 20A through Livonia. Continue east past Route 15A. Turn south on Canadice Hill Road. Pass Ross Road. Canadice Hill Road will turn to gravel. Turn left at the sign "Harriet Hollister Spencer Memorial Recreation Area" and park in the parking area on the left.
N42º 41.673 - W77º 31.507
Alternative Parking: Along the loop at the end of the park road.
N42º 41.3490 - W77º 30.7932
Length: Over 10 miles of trails
Difficulty: 👣 👣 👣

Surface: Dirt trails
Trail Markings: Some cross-country ski trail signs (blue squares, black diamonds) and some brown and yellow trail-name signs
Uses: 🚶 🚲 🎿 🐎 🛷

Dogs: OK on leash
Contact: N.Y.S. Office of Parks, Recreation and Historic Preservation
Stony Brook State Park
10820 Route 36 South, Dansville, NY 14437
(585) 335-8111

High in the hills, between Canadice Lake and Honeoye Lake, this area is treasured by cross-country skiers because it often has snow when the surrounding area doesn't. The trails in this park are constructed, maintained, and groomed in winter by volunteers from the N.Y.S. Section 5 Ski League. The rest of the year the trails are lesser used and are a wonderland for hikers and off-road bikers.

A trail parallel to the park road offers a grand view of Honeoye Lake in the valley. A bench labeled "A favorite place of Todd Ewers" is available to sit and savor the view.

A view of Honeoye Lake from the trails in Harriet Hollister.

Within the woods you'll follow 8-foot-wide dirt trails. Sometimes narrow trails veer off as shortcuts or deer paths, but stay on the wide trails.

Big Oak - Bear Cub Loop

Hiking Time: 1 hour loop
Length: 1.9-mile loop (darkened trail)

The Big Oak and Bear Cub Trail loop rambles through deep woods and is shady and cool on a hot day. We once watched a family of baby raccoons play along the trail. The southeast section of this loop is steep.

Trail Directions
• From the parking area, head north on the trail.
• Bear left on Big Oak Trail past a blue, "more difficult" cross-country ski sign. (Bear Cub Run is to the right.)
• Follow the trail around, staying on the main trail.
• Pass a narrow woods trail to the right.
• Toward the top of a hill, bear right, then take a quick right turn. You're now on Bear Cub Run. (Straight leads to the park road.)
• At the "T," turn left to return to the parking area.

Date Hiked: _____

Notes:

Fox Run - Raccoon Run - Sidewinder Loop

Hiking Time: 1.5 hour loop
Length: 2.6-mile loop (darkened trail)

Take a longer hike through these pristine woods by combining several trails. The trails are poorly marked, but a few signs along the way can act as waymarkers.

Trail Directions
• Park along the loop at the end of the park road.
• Walk back down the road to find the first trail to the right (E), labeled Fox Run.
• Follow Fox Run as it winds, passing a "bear trap" sign.
• When the trail meets Raccoon Run, turn left.
• Take the first left onto Sidewinder at the sign "Sidewinder - one way" (N42° 41.123 - W77° 30.723). As the name implies, this trail will wind.
• Pass a "viper" sign at N42° 41.092 - W77° 30.628.
• Pass a bench at the base of a steep hill at N42° 41.022 - W77° 30.548.
• At the "T" turn left.
• Continue straight through a trail junction.
• At the next "T," turn right.
• Pass a trail to the right, then one to the left. Follow the trail downhill to a grassy area.
• Cross the grass to return to the parking loop.

Date Hiked: _____

Notes:

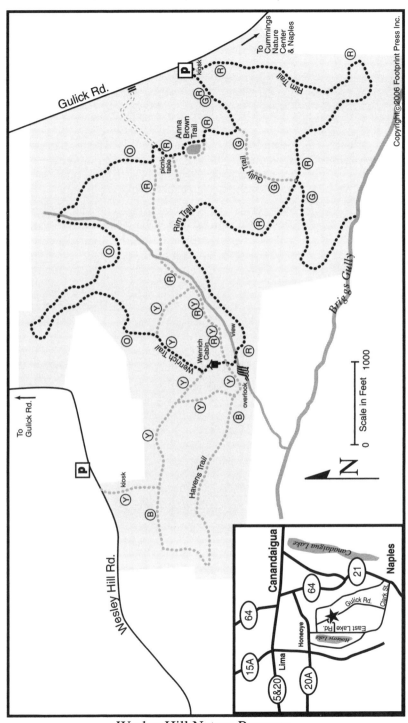

Wesley Hill Nature Preserve

7.

Wesley Hill Nature Preserve

Location: South Bristol, east of Honeoye Lake, Ontario County

Directions: From Route 20A, east of Honeoye Lake, turn south onto East Lake Road. Turn left onto Pine Hill Road. Turn right to stay on Pine Hill Road, following the signs for Cumming Nature Center. Pine Hill Road will become Gulick Road. Pass Wesley Hill Road, then watch right for a gravel parking area marked by a yellow and brown sign "Wesley Hill Nature Preserve."
N42° 43.452 - W77° 28.067

Alternative Parking: From Gulick Road, turn right onto Wesley Hill Road. In 1 mile watch right for a gravel parking area.
N42° 43.644 - W77° 29.071

Hiking Time: 2 hour loop

Length: 4-mile loop (darkened trails)
5.6 miles total trails

Difficulty: 👣👣 to 👣👣👣👣

Surface: Dirt trails

Trail Markings: Colored blazes

Uses: 🚶 🎿

Dogs: OK on leash

Contact: Finger Lakes Land Trust
202 E. Court Street, Ithaca, NY 14850
(607) 275-9487   www.fllt.org

This high-elevation piece of heaven was purchased by the Finger Lakes Land Trust in 1999 from the children of Rochester-area artists John C. Wenrich, James Havens and Colburn Dugan, who had used the area for peace, quiet, and contemplation. Thanks to their wish to protect this land for future generations, we can all enjoy its serenity. Another parcel was added to the preserve when the Humane Society of Rochester and Monroe County sold a plot to the Finger Lakes Land Trust that had been donated to them by Anna V. Brown. A bargain price and a generous anonymous donor helped seal the deal. The preserve now encompasses 359 acres and includes old-growth forests, fields, wetlands, streams, ponds, and deep gorges.

Hike through the stately old-growth forest of white pine, hemlock, oak, hickory and maple, to the serenade of song birds on the Rim Trail. Let your mind drift back to the time before white men settled this region and panthers, cougars, mountain lions and bears roamed freely. Follow the Gully Trail down to a picturesque spot in Briggs Gully where the water slides over scallops of shale. On a summer day, plan to get wet splashing in the water or sitting in the small chutes. Take a picnic and enjoy a respite near the pond on the Anna Brown Trail. Stop at the Wenrich cabin, built in the 1920s, to add your comments to the logbook kept on the porch. Since 2001 it has been collecting the preserve's recent history. Or, start on the Havens Trail where farmland is being reclaimed by a young forest and hike east to view the succession to old-growth.

Come in spring when wildflowers are in profusion. We hiked once in June when the trails were alive with toads hopping about. Or, come when the leaves are off the trees for sweeping views of the hills surrounding Honeoye Lake's southern end.

Trails:

Name	Blaze	Difficulty	Distance
Gully Trail	Green	4 boots	0.5 mile
Rim Trail	Red	3 boots	1.4 mile
Anna Brown Trail	Red	2 boots	0.7 mile
Wenrich Loop	Yellow	2 boots	1.6 mile
Orange Trail	Orange	2 boots	1.5 mile
Havens Trail	Blue	3 boots	0.8 mile

Trail Directions
- From the Gulick Road parking area, head south on the red trail.
- When the green trail intersects, turn left to hike down to Briggs Gully, then return to this same spot and keep heading northwest on the red trail.
- When the yellow trail intersects, hike past Wenrich cabin to the trail behind it and follow the yellow trail to the right.
- Turn left onto the orange trail.
- Turn left onto the red trail and follow it back to the parking lot. It doesn't matter which side of the pond you hike around.

Date Hiked: _____

Notes:

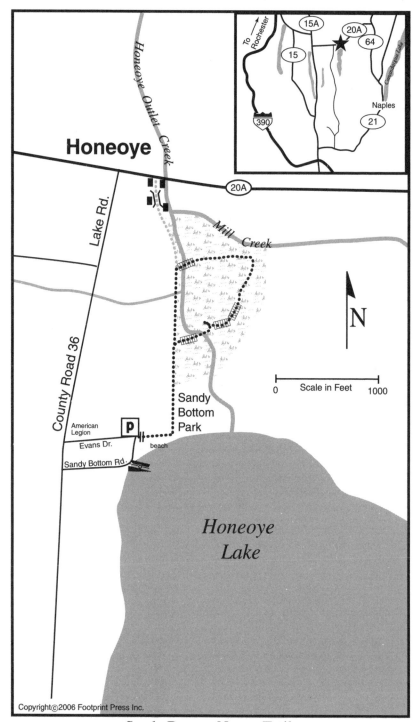

Sandy Bottom Nature Trail

8.

Sandy Bottom Nature Trail

Location: Sandy Bottom Park at the north end of Honeoye Lake, Ontario County
Directions: From Route 20A in the hamlet of Honeoye, head south on County Road 36 (Lake Road). Pass the American Legion Hall and turn left to enter Sandy Bottom Park. Park in the parking lot before the red metal gates.
N42° 47.050 - W77° 30.935
Alternate Parking: Between Aces Restaurant and Bird Haven on Route 20A.
Hiking Time: 30 minute loop
Length: 0.8-mile loop
Difficulty:

Surface: Boardwalk and grass paths
Trail Markings: None
Uses:

Dogs: Pets prohibited
Contact: Town of Richmond
8690 Main Street, P.O. Box 145, Honeoye, NY 14471
(585) 229-5757

Here's a special treat. A raised boardwalk has been erected over the Honeoye Outlet Creek and its wetlands, offering a gorgeous view at the north end of Honeoye Lake. We walked the trail in early spring and saw a loon paddling on the flooded wetlands and enjoyed the sights and sounds of many other birds. A variety of waterfowl, killdeers, kingfishers, hawks, owls and songbirds are all plentiful here. A careful observer may spot a raccoon, rabbit, woodchuck, deer, beaver, muskrat, or even mink or otter.

Sandy Bottom Park offers a swimming beach, boat launch, outhouses, ball fields and a skate park.

Trail Directions
• From the parking area, pass the red metal gates and head left toward the "Nature Trail" sign.

• Turn right when you reach the boardwalk.
• At the end of the boardwalk and trail loop, turn left to return to the parking area.

    Date Hiked: _____

    Notes:

The boardwalk over Honeoye Outlet Creek.

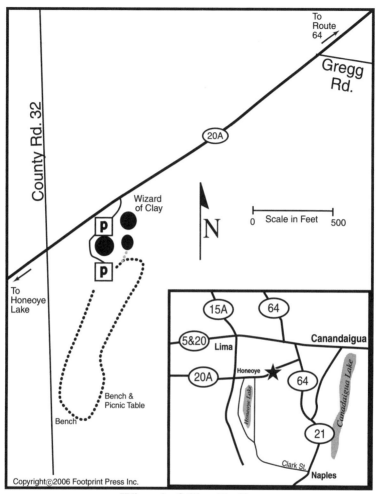

County Rd. 32

To Route 64

Gregg Rd.

20A

Wizard of Clay

P
P

To Honeoye Lake

N

Scale in Feet
0   500

Bench & Picnic Table

Bench

15A
64
5&20   Lima
Canandaigua
20A   Honeoye
64
Honeoye Lake
Canandaigua Lake
21
Clark St.
Naples

Copyright©2006 Footprint Press Inc.

Wizard of Clay Trail

9.

Wizard of Clay Trail

Location:	7851 Route 20A, between Honeoye and Canandaigua Lakes, Ontario County
Directions:	From Routes 5&20, west of Canandaigua, head south on Route 20A. Wizard of Clay is a collection of geodesic dome buildings on Route 20A near the corner of County Road 32. Park in the back, near the wooden sign "Nature Trail." N42o 48.6842 - W77o 27.7722
Hiking Time:	15 minute loop
Length:	0.5-mile loop
Difficulty:	👢👢 👢👢
Surface:	Woodland path
Trail Markings:	None
Uses:	🚶
Dogs:	OK
Contact:	The Wizard of Clay Pottery
	7851 Route 20A, Bloomfield, NY 14469
	(585) 229-2980 www.wizardofclay.com

The Wizard of Clay is an active workshop and retail store for handcrafted pottery, much of it sporting unique leaf inlays called Bristoleaf® design. Browse the shop, watch the wizard at work, then go for a walk.

The trail is a 4-foot-wide mowed swath through the woods. It heads uphill to form a horseshoe shape on the hillside. Clay (of course) placards identify some of the plants you pass along the way.

Trail Directions
- From the rear parking area, head under the wooden "Hiking Trail" sign.
- Follow the obvious trail as it heads uphill then loops back down to the parking area.

Date Hiked: _____

Notes:

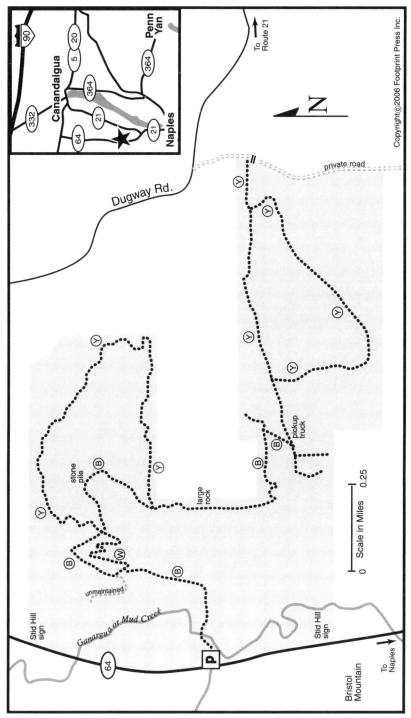

Stid Hill Multiple Use Area

10.

Stid Hill Multiple Use Area

Location: Bristol, Ontario County
Parking: The Stid Hill parking area on Route 64, 1.7 miles
                   south of Dugway Road (bottom of the hill), just past
                   the DEC "Stid Hill" sign. N42º 45.930 - W77º 24.364
Alternative Parking: Along Dugway Road, 2.0 miles from Route 64 (top
                   of the hill), where a square yellow sign on a tree up a
                   steep dirt road reads "Unauthorized Vehicles
                   Prohibited." Below it is a round, yellow DEC marker.
                   N42º 45.986 - W77º 22.739
Hiking Time: 2 hour loop
Length: 3.4-mile loop (darkened trail)
                   6.5 miles total trails
Difficulty: 👣 👣 👣 👣
Surface: Dirt trail
Trail Markings: 3"round, yellow DEC markers, colored blazes
Uses: 🚶 🚴
Facilities: None
Dogs: OK
Admission: Free, open June 1 through late fall
Contact: New York State DEC
                   6274 East Avon-Lima Road, Avon, NY 14414
                   (585) 226-2466

                   Rochester Bicycling Club
                   PO Box 10100, Rochester, NY 14610
                   www.rochesterbicyclingclub.org

Stid Hill, as the name implies, sits on the side of a hill. The area, opposite Bristol Mountain Ski Resort, is comprised of 3 tracts of land totalling 740 acres. At one time, Stid Hill was productive sheep and cattle grazing land. The livestock are gone. Left behind are steep hills, ravines, gullies, gorges, woods, and open fields that provide varied habitat for wildlife.

Included in the wildlife you'll find on Stid Hill are mountain biking enthusiasts. Members of the Rochester Bicycling Club and the National Mountain Bike Patrol created, maintain, and patrol the trails you'll hike. Don't let that deter you. The trails are in great shape, and we thoroughly enjoy hiking here.

Trail Directions
- From the Route 64 parking area, follow the mowed-grass blue-blazed-trail and cross a bridge over Ganargua Creek.
- At the white trail, turn right to head uphill.
- Continue straight onto the yellow trail.
- At the blue trail, turn left.
- Follow the blue trail all the way back to the parking area.

Date Hiked: _____
Notes:

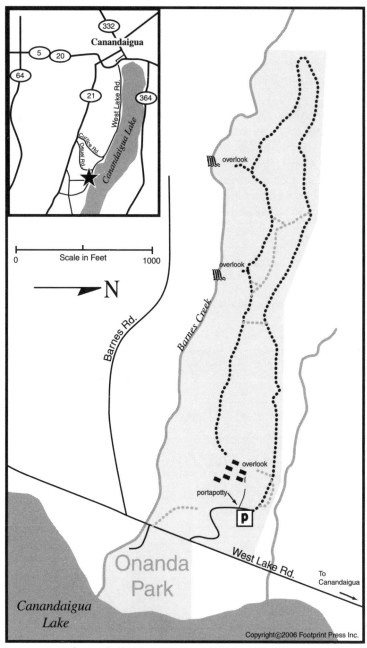

Onanda Park - Upland Hiking Trail

11.

Onanda Park - Upland Hiking Trail

Location:	The west side of Canandaigua Lake, Ontario County
Directions:	West Lake Road, 7 miles south of Canandaigua, south of Deuel Road. Enter the park on the west side of the road, away from the lake. Follow the park road uphill to the upper parking area.
	N42º 47.0477 - W77º 18.9118
Hiking Time:	45 minute loop
Length:	1.5-mile loop (darkened trail)
	1.75 miles total trails
Difficulty:	👣 👣 👣 👣
Surface:	Dirt trails
Trail Markings:	None, but easy-to-follow
Uses:	🚶
Dogs:	Pets NOT allowed
Admission:	Free (on the west side of the park)
Contact:	Onanda Park
	West Lake Road, Canandaigua, NY 14424
	(585) 394-0315 www.townofcanandaigua.org

Onanda Park was first a YWCA camp dating from 1919, then Camp Good Days and Special Times, which offered a respite to children with cancer. It became a public park in 1989 through a joint effort of New York State and the city of Canandaigua in an attempt to improve recreational opportunities and swimming access along Canandaigua Lake. Today the park covers 80 acres of land: 7 acres along the lake and 73 acres across West Lake Road, which is where you'll find the hiking trails.

Cabins, pavilions, and meeting facilities are available for rent within the park, mostly along the lakeshore. There are also a beach, fishing pier, picnic facilities, playgrounds, basketball, volleyball, and tennis courts on the lakeshore side. Admission is charged on the lakeshore side (free on the uphill side). The word Onanda derives from the Indian word for tall fir or pine tree, a symbol of simplicity and strength.

The trails wind up the hillside through the woods to observation platforms overlooking the deep gorge and waterfalls of Barnes Creek, that plummet over rock ledges.

Trail Directions
•Head uphill under the wooden sign "Upland Hiking Trail."
•Follow the wide, main trail around the perimeter.
•On the way back downhill, take the side trails to the 2 overlook points to view waterfalls below in Barnes Creek.

Date Hiked: _____

Notes:

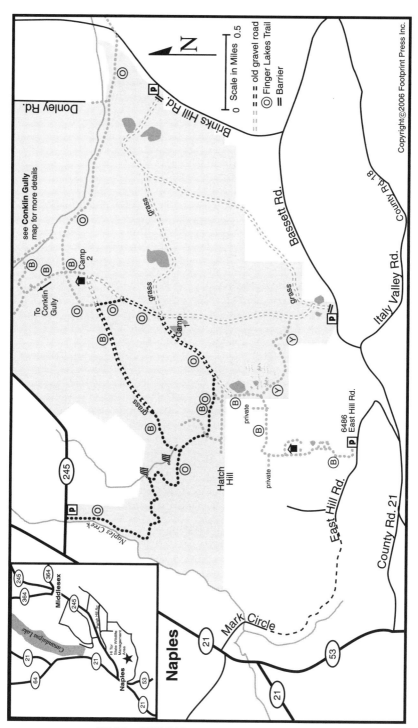

Hi Tor Wildlife Management Area

12.

Hi Tor Wildlife Management Area

Location:	Naples, south end of Canandaigua Lake, Ontario and Yates Counties
Directions:	From Route 21 (Main Street, Naples), turn east on Route 245. After crossing the Naples Creek bridge, park on the right in front of DEC near the sign "Naples Field Operations." N42º 37.557 - W77º 23.397

Alternative Parking: 6486 East Hill Road, N42º 35.875 - W77º 22.820
Alternative Parking: Bassett Road N42º 35.9864 - W77º 21.8018
Alternative Parking: Brinks Hill Road N42º 37.0570 - W77º 20.0449

Hiking Time:	3 hour loop
Length:	5.1-mile loop (darkened trails)
	17 miles total trails
Difficulty:	👣 👣 👣 👣
Surface:	Dirt trails
Trail Markings:	Some trails are color blazed
Uses:	🚶 🚴 ⛷ (Note: the orange-blazed Finger Lakes Trail is for hiking only.)
Dogs:	OK on leash
Contact:	Hi Tor Wildlife Management Area
	N.Y.S. Department of Environmental Conservation
	6274 East Avon-Lima Road, Avon, NY 14414
	(585) 226-2466 www.dec.state.ny.us
	Finger Lakes Trail Conference
	6111 Visitor Center Rd., Mt. Morris, NY 14510
	(585) 658-9320 www.fingerlakestrail.org

Hi Tor (sometimes spelled High Tor) is an old English word meaning high, craggy hill or peak. You'll agree with the "high" part as you climb steeply up Hatch Hill. The crags are the sharp gullies and eroded cliffs which cross this hill, making it scenic and physically challenging.

This hike is in Hi Tor Wildlife Management Area, a complex of 6,100 acres of hills, woods, and marshlands managed by the Department of Environmental Conservation (DEC). The majority of the recommended hike follows the Bristol Hills Branch of the Finger Lakes Trail (orange-

A view of Canandaigua Lake from Hi Tor.

blazed) as it crosses through Hi Tor, with a return loop on a blue-blazed trail.

The Bristol Hills Branch of the Finger Lakes Trail is a spur trail, which runs for 54 miles from Ontario County Park in the north until it meets the main Finger Lakes Trail at Mitchellsville (near the southern end of Keuka Lake). It makes a great five-day backpacking trip. The main Finger Lakes Trail runs for 557 miles between the Allegheny Mountains and the Catskill Mountains. Information and maps on all segments of the Finger Lakes Trail can be purchased from the Finger Lakes Trail Conference.

Prepare for a strenuous climb as you begin this hike. The trail switch-backs up Hatch Hill for 0.5 mile before following old logging roads on more level terrain. Most of the route is deep in the woods or under a tree canopy. A section on the blue-blazed trail is an old logging road which is wide and exposed to the sun. You have the option of continuing on the logging road (leaving the Finger Lakes Trail) for a short while on a side trip to a viewpoint, overlooking Canandaigua Lake in the valley far below.

You can also combine this trail with the Conklin Gully Trail (hike #13) for a strenuous 6-mile loop.

Camping is not allowed in Conklin Gully or in the Hi Tor Wildlife Management Area except by organized groups during non-hunting seasons with a written permit from the DEC Regional Wildlife Manager in Avon.

Trail Directions

•From the parking area on Route 245, head toward the brown kiosk next to Naples Creek. The trail begins on a grass swath along the east side of Naples Creek. Walk south on this orange-blazed grass path.

•At 1.1 miles, reach the blue trail intersection. The blue trail will be your return loop. Continue uphill on the trail which is now blazed orange and blue.

•Reach a "T" where the blue trail veers off. (The blue trail heads south to a parking area on East Hill Road.) Turn left on the old logging road, following the orange blazes.

•At 2 miles, reach an intersection and turn left to stay on the orange-blazed trail. This old logging road continues to head downhill gradually.

•At 2.1 miles, watch for brown posts on both sides of the trail. This flags the left turn of the Finger Lakes Trail into the woods. Turn left and follow the orange blazes into the woods.

[Alternate Route: If you want to reach a vista of Canandaigua Lake, continue on the logging road to where it takes a sharp bend left. This is the site of "camp 2" (camping is not allowed) and the vista. Return to the logging road and follow it as it bends left (W). It will pass the intersection of the orange trail and by continuing straight, you'll be on the blue-blazed return loop.

Or, by following the blue-blazed trail north out of camp 2, you can connect to Conklin Gully Trail #13.]

•You'll be going downhill through the woods on the orange-blazed trail.

•At 2.3 miles, meet the logging road. At this point, leave the orange trail (which continues straight) and turn left onto the blue trail (the logging road) heading downhill.

•The old logging road turns to a grass path. At 2.7 miles, the wide portion ends, and the blue trail turns left into the woods. N42º 37.176 - W77º 22.470

•At 2.9 miles, cross a stream gully. Then up a short hill to a "T" with the orange trail. Turn right (NW) and follow the orange trail downhill to the parking area.

Date Hiked: _____

Notes:

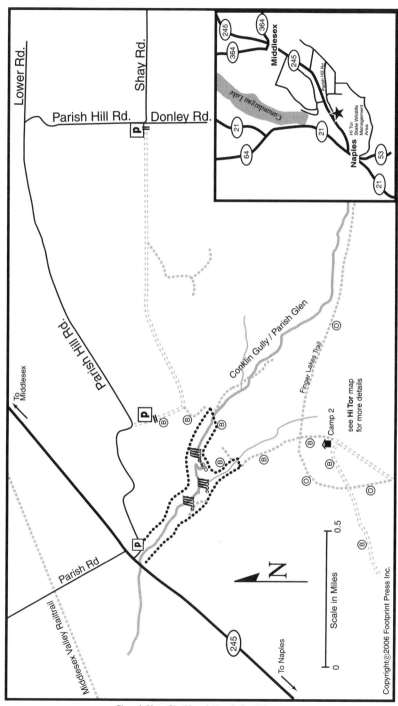

Conklin Gully / Parish Glen

13.

Conklin Gully / Parish Glen

Location: Naples, south end of Canandaigua Lake, Yates County

Directions: From Route 21 (Main Street, Naples), turn east onto Route 245. Turn right (E) onto Parish Hill Road. Soon a small green and white DEC "Public Hunting Grounds" sign will be on the right. Park along Parish Hill Road near this sign. N43° 38.104 - W77° 21.987

Alternative Parking: A parking area to the right, further east on Parish Hill Road. N42° 38.084 - W77° 21.431

Alternative Parking: At the corner of Shay Road & Parish Hill Road. N42° 38.112 - W77° 20.183

Hiking Time: 1 hour loop

Length: 1.6-mile loop

Difficulty: 👣 👣 👣 👣

Surface: Dirt trails

Trail Markings: Most of the trail is unmarked. The trail from Parish Hill Road, through Conklin Gully and into Hi Tor Management Area is blue-blazed.

Uses: 🚶

Dogs: OK on leash

Contact: Hi Tor Wildlife Management Area
N.Y.S. Department of Environmental Conservation
6274 East Avon-Lima Road, Avon, NY 14414
(585) 226-2466 www.dec.state.ny.us

The locals call this ravine Parish Glen. The Parish family settled in the Naples area in 1789, on roughly a thousand acres that included Parish Glen and Parish Hill (now part of Hi Tor). No one knows where the name Conklin Gully came from, other than that it shows up on USGS topographical maps.

Letchworth does not have the only spectacular gorge in the Genesee Valley. Water rushing off Parish Hill on its way to Naples Creek and Canandaigua Lake dug an equally spectacular, but smaller trench through the earth. Prepare to do some climbing to find it. This hike begins and ends with steep climbs. But the views of the gorge and waterfalls are well worth the climb. At the eastern end you'll cross two branches of the creek which merge to form the Conklin Gully gorge. The view draws you in but be wary. Don't go near the edges of the gorge – the banks often overhang with no support underneath. Because of this, Conklin Gully isn't the best hike for small children. There are no guardrails.

The hike is not to be missed, but consider taking along water shoes and seeing the gorge from water level after your walk. The rocks are slippery, so take care.

Camping is not allowed in Conklin Gully or in the Hi Tor Wildlife Management Area except by organized groups during non-hunting seasons by written permit from the DEC Regional Wildlife Manager in Avon.

Trail Directions
•From the pull-off area on Parish Hill Road, with the creek to your right, follow any of the herdpaths on the left that head sharply uphill.
•Continue southeast along the edge of the gorge.
•At 0.5 mile, meet the blue-blazed trail. Turn right (S) and begin following the blue blazes. (Left heads to the alternate parking area on Parish Hill Road and to the abandoned road to Shay Road.)
•Continue following the blue blazes until you've crossed two creek branches.
•Shortly, reach a "T" with a wide trail. Leave the blue trail at this point and turn right (NW).
[The blue trail turns left and heads deeper into Hi Tor. Continue following the blue trail if you want to connect this hike with the Hi Tor Wildlife Management Area (hike #12) for a strenuous 6-mile loop.]
•Pass a clearing on your left. Continue straight into a pine woods.
•As the trail heads downhill, Conklin Gully will be on your right.
•Reach a "Y." You can go in either direction. The trail to the left stays inland. The trail to the right follows the gorge rim. The two trails merge in 0.1 mile.
•At 1.6 miles, reach Route 245. Turn right, cross the bridge, then turn right on Parish Hill Road to return to the parking area.

Date Hiked: _____
Notes:

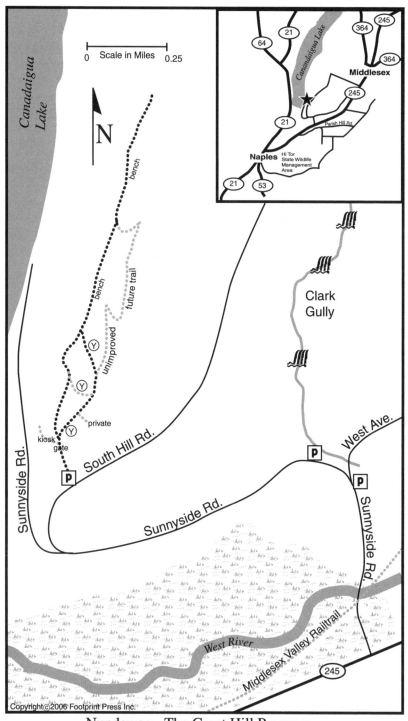

Nundawao - The Great Hill Preserve

14.

Nundawao — The Great Hill Preserve

Location:	The southeast side of Canandaigua Lake, Yates County
Directions:	From Naples, head northeast on Route 245. Turn left onto Sunnyside Road. Keep left past West Ave., then take the next right onto South Hill Road. In 0.7 mile watch left for a sign "Nundawao - Finger Lakes Land Trust." There's a minimal parking area with room for 1 or 2 cars. N42° 39.600 - W77° 20.943
Hiking Time:	1 hour loop
Length:	1.9-mile loop (darkened trail) 2.2 miles total trails
Difficulty:	👣👣 main trail, 👣👣👣 yellow-blazed side trails
Surface:	Main trail is grass (sporadically mowed), yellow-blazed side trails are dirt and forest leaf litter
Trail Markings:	None on main trail, yellow blazes on side trails
Uses:	🚶 🎿
Dogs:	OK on leash
Contact:	Finger Lakes Land Trust 202 East Court Street, Ithaca, NY 14850 (607) 275-9487 www.fllt.org

In 2001, Thomas and Sandra Hansen of Middlesex donated 220 acres of land overlooking Canandaigua Lake to the Finger Lakes Land Trust. This was followed by a donation from James & Ellen Fralick of a 5-acre inholding. Together, these generous donations helped to preserve a scenic piece of South Hill as well as an important part of the Canandaigua Lake watershed.

This parcel was heavily logged for its hardwoods in the 19th century, but the forest has rebounded with a tall canopy of oaks, hickories, maple, and ash. The terrain was too steep to ever have been farmed. Before 19th century loggers, this was the birthplace of the Seneca Indians. Their fort, Nundawao, sat atop South Hill.

The steep hillside with its soft soils, is accessible from an almost level old logging road off South Hill Road. Canandaigua Lake sits 500 feet below.

Come visit in fall or winter when leaves are off the trees for the best lake views. This is a great place to look for birds. Listen for the ethereal song of the hermit thrush or the short twitters of the yellow-rumped warbler. In the winter, look for tracks left by wild turkey, fox and deer. Even on a summer hike, we spotted a red fox.

Be aware that portions of the yellow-blazed trail are on private property and may be rerouted in the future.

Trail Directions
•Follow the 8-foot-wide grass path from the parking area.
•Near the kiosk, turn right and head uphill on the yellow-blazed trail.
•Pass a yellow-blazed connector path to the left and continue following a yellow-blazed trail until it heads downhill and meets the main trail.
•Turn right and follow the main trail to its end.
•Turn around and follow the main trail back to the parking area.

Date Hiked: _____
Notes:

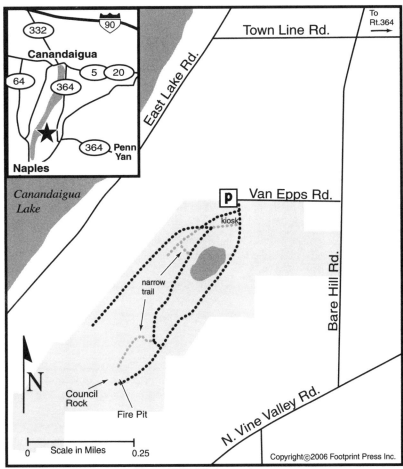

Bare Hill Unique Area

15.

Bare Hill Unique Area

Location:	East side of Canandaigua Lake, Yates County
Directions:	From Canandaigua, head south on Route 364. Turn right (W) on Town Line Road, left (S) on Bare Hill Road, and right (W) on Van Epps Road. Pass a brown and yellow DEC sign, "Bare Hill Unique Area." Park along the side of Van Epps Road where it dead-ends. N42° 44.802 - W77° 18.163
Hiking Time:	1.75 hour loop
Length:	3.1-mile loop (darkened trail)
	2.3 miles total trails
Difficulty:	👣 👣 👣
Surface:	Mowed field and gravel trail
Trail Markings:	None
Uses:	🚶 🚴 🎿
Dogs:	OK on leash
Contact:	N.Y.S. Department of Environmental Conservation
	7291 Coon Road, Bath, NY 14810
	(607) 776-2165 ext. 29 www.dec.state.ny.us

Bare Hill rises 865 feet above Canandaigua Lake and provides awe-inspiring views of the lake and valley. It also lives up to its name. The Department of Environmental Conservation (DEC) mows around the trees on the summit, keeping this hilltop bare.

You will walk land where the Genundowa Festival of Lights originated. Genundowa was the name of a Seneca village near Bare Hill. Each year in early September, the Seneca Elders and the tribes Keepers would light a large fire on top of Bare Hill as part of the Seneca Autumn Ceremony of Thanksgiving for a successful harvest. This fire was followed by smaller fires along the lake, resulting in a ring of light as a gesture of Indian unity.

Seneca history is hidden in legend. One legend says that the first Seneca settlement occurred in Naples Valley around 1400. Other legends assert that they came from the Adirondack area or from Montreal, either following

Council Rock sits atop Bare Hill.

game or to escape warring tribes. In either case, by the 1600s the Seneca Nation numbered over 10,000.

Seneca folklore has an explanation for the tree-less nature of Bare Hill. Legend says that while out canoeing one day, a Seneca youth found a brightly colored snake which he adopted as his pet. The boy fed the serpent insects, frogs and small mammals. As the serpent grew, bigger animals were supplied. Over time, it became so large that the boy, now a warrior and skilled hunter, had to request the assistance of the village in obtaining sufficient food. The small, beautiful snake had become a ravenous monster.

The villagers began to fear the serpent when food supplies dwindled, and they planned to escape to a new fortified village on a hill to the north. The monster serpent appeared, coiled its great body around the village and swallowed all but two children, a brother and sister who did not follow the villagers in their attempt to escape.

In a dream, a spirit instructed the boy to kill the snake by shooting an arrow in a scale behind its eye. The boy's shot was successful, but death did not come immediately. The serpent's mammoth body writhed and twisted, its long tail viciously lashed the hillside, smashing trees and bushes until the hillside was swept clean. As the serpent plunged down the hill, the heads of its human victims were disgorged. Finally the great serpent fell into the lake. Today, round stones found in the area are known to geologists as septaria and to local residents as Indian heads.

Around 1570, five Seneca tribes united into the League of Five Nations, later called the Iroquois Confederacy. Historians call this early government the "greatest achievement of Stone Age man" because of its extensive code of laws. Council Rock at the summit of Bare Hill was the traditional site of the Seneca Indian council fires.

Trail Description
- From Van Epps Road, pass the yellow metal gate.
- Soon the trail branches at a "Y." A kiosk describes the history of the area. Bear right at the "Y."
- Bear or turn right at each trail junction.
- At 0.7 mile, the trail dead-ends. Turn around and retrace your path.
- Continue straight through the first junction, then turn right at the second.
- The trail bends left as you continue steeply uphill.
- At 1.8 miles reach a "T." Turn right.
- The trail dead-ends at Council Rock with a commanding view of Canandaigua Lake.
- Turn around and head down the hill, bearing right at each junction along the way.

Date Hiked: _____

Notes:

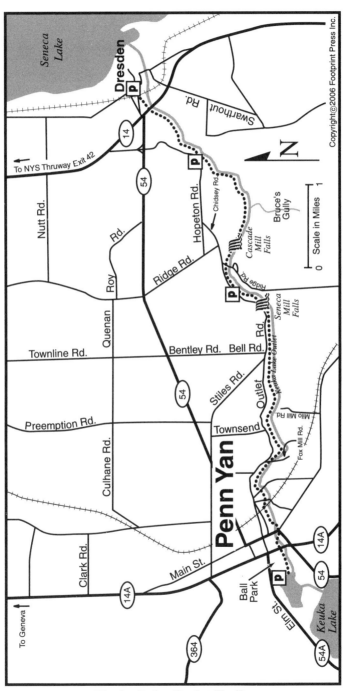

Keuka Lake Outlet Trail

16.

Keuka Lake Outlet Trail

Location: Dresden to Penn Yan, Yates County
Directions: From Route 14 south along the west side of Seneca Lake, turn left (E) at Route 54 heading toward Main Street, Dresden. There is a Citgo gas station and the Crossroads Ice Cream Shop at the corner. At the Crossroads Ice Cream Shop, take an immediate right onto Seneca Street. Parking is on your right just before the railroad tracks. N42º 40.8619 - W76º 57.5206
Alternative Parking: Penn Yan, Marsh Development Project, Little League Baseball, on Route 54A (Elm Street) N42º 39.5139 - W77º 3.6321
Alternative Parking: Outlet Road N42º 39.9181 - W77º 0.0787
Alternative Parking: Hopeton Road N42º 40.2913 - W76º 58.2801
Hiking Time: 4 hours one way
Length: 6.8 miles one way
Distances Between Parking Areas:
Dresden to Hopeton Road: 1.0 miles
Hopeton Road to Outlet Road: 2.0 miles
Outlet Road to Route 54A: 3.8 miles
Difficulty: 👣 👣
Surface: Dirt (western end is paved)
Trail Markings: Green and white metal "Trail" signs
Uses:
🚶 🚵 🎿 🛷 🐎
Dogs: OK on leash
Contact: Friends of the Outlet
P.O. Box 65, Dresden, NY 14441
www.keukaoutlettrail.net

The strip of land you will be walking from Seneca Lake to Keuka Lake is steeped in history. You'll see evidence of places and events from several bygone eras as you walk westward.

In the middle of the nineteenth century, two fingers of water connected the 274-foot drop between Keuka and Seneca Lakes, the outlet to power

Rest awhile and enjoy Seneca Mill Falls.

mills, and the Crooked Lake Canal for boat traffic. A dam and guardhouse in Penn Yan controlled the water flow to both. The outlet, which still carries water from one lake to the next, was formed by a ground fault in the Tully limestone allowing water to run between the two lakes. Along its banks, you'll see remnants of the many mills which once harnessed the waterpower.

The first white settlers arrived in this area around 1788, attracted by the reliable water source at the outlet. In 1789 Seneca Mill was built along the raging waters of Keuka Lake outlet to grind flour with a 26-foot, overshot flywheel. From then until 1827, a small religious group called the Society of Universal Friends built 12 dams and many mills that helped make the area a thriving community. The mills and shops produced flour (gristmills), lumber (sawmills), tool handles, linseed oil, plaster, and liquor (distilleries). There were two triphammer forges, eight fulling and carding mills, tanneries, and weavers making cotton and wool cloth. By 1835, 30 to 40 mills were in operation. However, by 1900, only five mills remained, mainly making paper from straw. The last water-turbine mill ceased operation in 1968.

In 1833 New York State opened the Crooked Lake Canal to span the six miles between the two lakes and move farm products to eastern markets. The canal was four feet deep and had 28 wooden locks. It took a vessel six hours to journey through the canal. As business boomed in the mills, the state widened and deepened the canal and replaced the wooden locks with stone. But the canal lost money every year of its 44-year history, so in 1877 the state auctioned off all the machinery and stone. Only the towpath remained. In 1844 a railroad was built on the towpath. Initially operated by the Penn Yan and New York Railway Company, it eventually became part of the New York Central System. Railway men called it the "Corkscrew Railway" because of its countless twists and turns. The line operated until 1972 when the tracks were washed out by the flood from Hurricane Agnes.

A local group interested in recreational use of the ravine convinced the town of Penn Yan to buy the property in 1981. Since then, it has been developed and maintained by a volunteer group called the Friends of the Outlet. Trail signs and outhouses were added along the route.

Reference Guides: Purchase an illustrated guide to the Keuka Lake Outlet for $1.00 from the Yates County Historian, 110 Court Street, Penn Yan, NY 14527. A packet of information on the history of the mill sites, canal, and railroad of the Keuka Lake Outlet is available for $3.00 at stores in Penn Yan.

Trail Directions
- The trail leads downhill from the back-right corner of the Dresden parking lot, heading west.
- Cross under the Route 14 bridge. The land you're on used to be the Dresden Mill Pond.
- The wetland to your right (north of the trail) is the old Crooked Lake Canal.
- Cross two wooden bridges.
- Notice the steep cliffs on both sides. Where the canal and outlet are close together was the location of Lock 3. Watch for the cement and rebar millstone.
- Cross a dirt road. This was Hopeton Road, which in the 1790s connected Geneva to Bath through the town of Hopeton. To your left you can still see remnants of the iron-pony, truss bridge over the outlet. The bridge was built in 1840 and rests on stone abutments. This area was once a community of mills. Hopeton Grist Mill was located just beyond the dirt road on the left. Nothing remains of it today.
- On your left is a pleasant rest area with large rocks where you can sit along the water.
- Across the outlet, Bruces Gully cascades water over three waterfalls to join the outlet. Eventually the Friends of the Outlet plan to build a hiking trail through the gully. The dark gray rock, which peels in thin layers, is Genesee shale.

- Pass a cement pillar on your right. The big "W" on the pillar signaled the train conductor to blow his whistle.
- At the two-mile point are the remains of the J.T. Baker Chemical Company, manufacturers of the pesticide carbine bisulfide until 1968. At one time, this was also the site of a gristmill and several paper mills.
- Here you'll see your first waterfall. The top step of the falls was the old dam, constructed in 1827 and the last of the 12 dams built along the outlet. Both Cascade Mill and Mallory's Mill used the water that was held back by this dam.
- Follow the wide gravel path through the building area.
- Pass old Kelly Tire buildings. The Friends of the Outlet renovated these buildings into the Alfred Jensen Memorial Visitor Center. It's a good place to stop if you need a restroom.
- Follow the green and white trail signs as the trail branches to the left.
- At 2.6 miles, cross the paved Ridge Road. In 1805 May's Mills stood at this site. It had a gristmill, a sawmill, and a post office. In the 1820s this area was home to a cotton factory, then a distillery.
- Continue along the outlet. Outlet Road parallels close to the trail.
- Just over a culvert is another cement post displaying a "W," then another cement marker with "D3" which told the conductor that Dresden was three miles away. This means that you're almost halfway to Penn Yan.
- Pass a parking lot off Outlet Road. The brick remnants on the right were once a factory that turned rags into paper.
- Look for the large rock between the trail and the outlet. A plaque on the side facing the outlet commemorates John Sheridan, a lawyer who negotiated the purchase of land for the Keuka Lake Outlet Preservation Area. The stone remnants across the outlet were once a forge. At one time a road crossed over the dam at this spot. Seneca Mill, the first mill site, was located at this falls, the largest falls on the outlet.
- On your right (away from the outlet) is a stone wall with a large round opening. This used to house a pipe to vent train smoke out of the valley.
- The machinery that remains at the top of the dam controlled water flow through a sluiceway. The original Friends Mill, a complex of paper and gristmills, was here. There's now a nice picnic pavilion here.
- The trail bears right through Lock 17, which was the downstream end of a series of four locks needed to maneuver the elevation drop.
- You're now walking in a ravine of the old canal bed. In May this segment of trail is lined with trillium. It's also an active beaver area.
- Pass another cement whistle sign on the right.

- The cement wall in the water is the end of a race from Milo Mills. The stagnant water on the left is the raceway. From here to Penn Yan was the most industrialized section of the outlet.
- A large brick chimney towers over the remains of a paper mill, built in 1890, burned in 1910, and then rebuilt. You can still see the 17-foot flywheel which used two miles of hemp cable and was run by a steam engine. The machinery was manufactured at the Rochester foundry at Brown's Race.
- At 4.4 miles, cross Milo Mill Road.
- Cross a bridge over a wood-lined sluice. This used to carry water to Shutt's Mill, which dates back to about 1850.
- A small side path immediately to the left leads to the ruins of Shutt's Mill. You can still see the stone vats from this paper mill that manufactured wallboard. Shutt's Mill burned in 1933. The first mill at this site was a sawmill built in 1812. It was followed by a wool mill, a gristmill, and a fulling mill. Beware of the poison ivy in the area.
- The waterfall on the far side of the outlet, just before a road and bridge, is outflow from the municipal sewage plant.
- Cross a road. Dibbles Mill used to make wooden wheels in this area.
- The green shed across the road on the right was a blacksmith shop from canal times (around 1838). The blacksmith specialized in shoeing mules.
- At 5.5 miles, cross paved Fox Mill Road. If you take a left on Fox Mill Road, then a quick right toward the outlet, you'll find remains from the Fox Mill which manufactured straw paper. The stone for the walls was moved here from the dismantled locks of Crooked Lake Canal around 1865.
- Pass a sign for St. John's Mill. Other than the sign, there's nothing to see. The mill used to be across the outlet.
- Cross paved Cherry Street. The trail becomes paved.
- Pass under a railroad trestle called "High Bridge." It was originally built of wood in 1850 and was rebuilt in 1890.
- The large circular hollow just after the trestle was once a turntable for the train.
- Pass signs for an exercise trail. After the chin-up bars on the right, a small path leads left to another cement railroad marker "D6," indicating six miles from Dresden.
- Reach the wooden bridge which served as a railroad trestle to Birkett Mills in 1824. Birkett Mills took their water turbines out in 1947.
- At 6.5 miles, pass under the Main Street (Penn Yan) bridge which was built in 1884 from canal stone. This area used to have the guardhouse

for the canal. The dam on the right is used to control the water level in Keuka Lake. The brown building you can see was a grain warehouse. At one time this section of trail was home to several woodworking factories, a cooperage, and a sash-and-blind factory.

•Pass through a park then cross the pedestrian bridge over the outlet.

•Continue through Penn Yan Recreation Complex on the paved path. You pass restrooms, a boat launch, tennis courts, and a small playground.

•Cross another wooden bridge over Sucker Brook.

•Pass through the athletic fields to the parking lot in Marsh Development Project on Route 54A.

Date Hiked: _____

Notes:

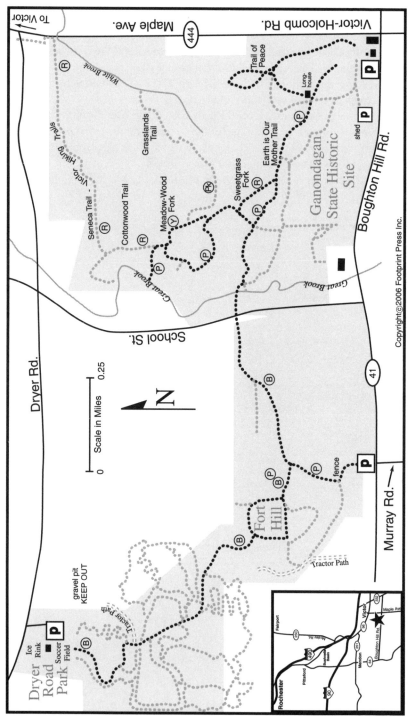

Ganondagan / Fort Hill / Dryer Road Park

17.

Ganondagan State Historic Site / Dryer Road Park

Location: Ganondagan State Historic Site, Boughton Hill Road, Victor, Ontario County

Directions: From Route 96 in Victor, turn south on Maple Avenue (State Route 444) then west on Boughton Hill Road (County Road 41), Ganondagan parking lot is on Boughton Hill Road near the corner of Victor-Holcomb Road.   N42° 57.685 - W77° 24.788

Alternative Parking: A parking area near the shed off Boughton Hill Road.   N42° 57.6800 - W77° 24.8447

Alternative Parking: The Fort Hill parking area on Boughton Hill Road.   N42° 57.670 - W77° 25.924

Uses:

Dogs: OK on leash

Contact: Ganondagan State Historic Site
P.O. Box 239, 1488 Victor-Holcomb Road
Victor, NY 14564-0239
(585) 924-5848   www.ganondagan.org

Once a major seventeenth-century Seneca town and its palisaded granary, Ganondagan is the only historic site, under the auspices of New York State Office of Parks, Recreation and Historic Preservation, that is dedicated to Native Americans. The town and its associated burial grounds on Boughton Hill were designated a National Historic Landmark in 1964. Fort Hill, the site of the town's granary, was placed on the National Register of Historic Places in 1966 because it was part of the French campaign of destruction in 1687. The Marquis de Denonville, Governor General of New France, led an army of 3,000 men from Canada against the Seneca in July, 1687, in an effort to annihilate the Seneca and eliminate them as competitors in the international fur trade.

The Seneca recall a much earlier time period, when a man referred to as the Peacemaker journeyed to their territory and met a woman known as Mother of Nations or Peace Mother. The Seneca know Ganondagan as the "Town of Peace," and revere and protect the burial site of the Mother of Nations near here.

Interpretive signs on the three main trails within Ganondagan teach the significance of plant life for the Seneca, Seneca customs and beliefs, features of the 30 acre granary at Fort Hill, and the events that took place at the granary. On July 14, 1987, Ganondagan was dedicated — 300 years to the day after Denonville destroyed life at Ganondagan.

In 1997 and 1998 a full-scale bark longhouse was constructed at Ganondagan based on extensive research of oral, archaeological, and historical records. The 65-foot long, 20-foot wide structure is stocked with artifacts and displays, showing not only how the Seneca lived, but their governmental and spiritual philosophies as well. When the peaceful Seneca inhabited Ganondagan, up to 20 families could have lived in each longhouse. Ganondagan was the largest Seneca town known to have existed. In the 17th century it had over 150 longhouses and approximately 4,500 residents. Hours that the longhouse is open for viewing vary throughout the year. Call (585) 924-5848 for the current schedule.

The visitor center at Ganondagan features an exhibit describing the Seneca clan system, a display of works by Seneca artists, and a twenty-seven minute video about the history of Ganondagan. The visitor center and gift shop are open May 15 through October 31, Wednesday through Sunday, 9 AM to 5 PM.

There are many options for walks at Ganondagan State Historic Site. Four options are described starting on the following page:

A statue of Seneca Indians guards the Longhouse.

Trail of Peace

Hiking Time:	15 minute loop
Length:	0.4-mile loop
Difficulty:	👞
Surface:	Mowed-grass path
Trail Markings:	None

Stay on top of the hill and walk the undulating mowed-grass paths of the Trail of Peace through open field for an easy 0.4-mile loop, and visit the replica longhouse.

Trail Directions
- From the parking area head north through the opening in the split-rail fence to cross a mowed-grass area toward a sign "Trail of Peace."
- Visit the longhouse, then continue north on the mowed-grass loop trails, passing interpretive signs.

    Date Hiked: _____

    Notes:

Earth Is Our Mother Trail

Hiking Time:	1.0 hour loop
Length:	1.9-mile loop
Difficulty:	👞 👞 👞
Surface:	Dirt path with boardwalks
Trail Markings:	Colored metal markers

Head into the woods for the more challenging Earth is Our Mother Trail.

Trail Directions
- From the parking area head north through the opening in the split-rail fence to cross a mowed-grass area toward a sign "Trail of Peace."
- Pass the longhouse. Head into the woods behind it, passing the silver and black "Ethnobotanical Trail" sign.

•Follow the purple marked trail outbound to Great Brook and take the yellow (Meadow-Wood Fork) and red (Sweetgrass Fork) marked segments on the return.

Date Hiked: _____

Notes:

Fort Hill Trail

Directions:	The grass parking area for Fort Hill will be on the north side of Boughton Hill Road near the corner of Murray Road. N42° 57.670 - W77° 25.924
Hiking Time:	30 minutes to hike (1 hour to hike & read the signs)
Length:	1-mile loop
Difficulty:	🥾 🥾 🥾
Surface:	Dirt and mowed-grass paths
Trail Markings:	Parts of the trail are marked purple & blue

The Fort Hill Trail takes you to the top of a plateau with sweeping views of valleys and hillsides across Victor. This was once the site of the picketed granary for Ganondagan where the winter supply of corn was stored. Forty interpretive signs give first-hand accounts of the mass destruction of the granary by the French campaign of 1687.

Trail Directions
• From the parking area head uphill (N) on the mowed path.
• Turn right and enter the woods through wooden fence posts.
• At 0.2 mile, cross a boardwalk. (To your left note the marsh area, once a spring used by the Seneca.)
• Turn left at the blue trail junction.
• At the top of the plateau, head either direction to walk the perimeter of the clearing. Read the interpretive signs along the way, and sit and enjoy the views of farmland in the valley below.
• Return to the parking area, downhill, via the same trail.

Date Hiked: _____

Notes:

Traverse to Dryer Road Park

Location:	Ganondagan State Historic Site on Boughton Hill Road to Dryer Road Park on Dryer Road, Victor, Ontario County
Directions:	From Route 96 in Victor, turn south on Maple Avenue (State Route 444), then west on Boughton Hill Road (County Road 41). Ganondagan parking lot is on Boughton Hill Road near the corner of Victor-Holcomb Road. N42º 57.685 - W77º 24.788
Alternative Parking:	Dryer Road Park on the south side of Dryer Road, between Cork Road and Malone Road. N42º 58.375 - W77º 26.416 The trail begins straight back (S) from the parking area, under a large oak tree.
Hiking Time:	1.5 hours one way
Length:	2.5 miles, one way (darkened trail)
Difficulty:	👣 👣 👣
Surface:	Woods paths and mowed-grass paths
Trail Markings:	The connector trail has blue markers
Uses:	🚶 🎿 Trails within Dryer Road Park: 🚴
Dogs:	OK on leash
Admission:	Free
Contact:	Town of Victor, Parks & Recreation
	85 East Main Street, Victor, NY 14564-1397
	www.victorny.org/parks

One of the Town of Victor's newest parks, Dryer Road Park is still under development. Today it offers a playground, soccer fields, a skating rink, restrooms, and a network of mountain biking trails. Best of all, it connects to Ganondagan State Historic Site and has a particularly scenic hiking trail with a view of downtown Rochester in the distance. Between Dryer Road Park and Fort Hill, the trail traverses the top of a plateau ridge. The side loops follow the perimeter of fields on top of the plateau, then drop down off the plateau.

Trail Directions

- From the Ganondagan parking area head north through the opening in the split-rail fence to cross a mowed-grass area toward a sign "Trail of Peace."

- Pass the longhouse. Head into the woods behind it, passing the silver and black "Ethnobotanical Trail" sign.
- Pass the red trail junction, then continue straight through the next junction, leaving the purple trail.
- Continue heading west to cross Great Brook and School Street.
- Follow the blue trail back uphill to the Fort Hill plateau.
- On top of Fort Hill, turn right, still following blue blazes and head into the woods.
- The blue trail will lead to the parking area in Dryer Road Park.

Date Hiked: _____

Notes:

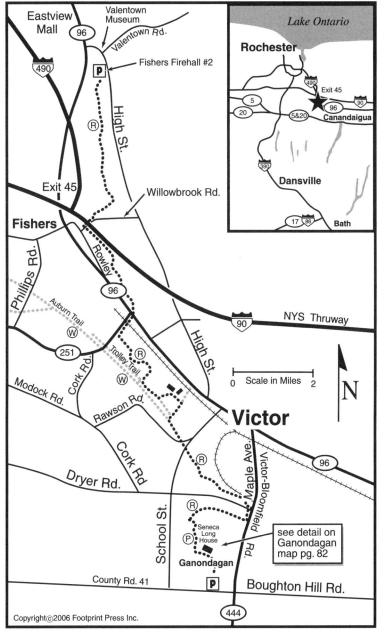

Seneca Trail

18.

Seneca Trail

Location:	Victor, Ontario County
Directions:	From New York State Thruway exit 45, head south on Route 96. In Victor, turn south on Maple Avenue (State Route 444). Turn west on Boughton Hill Road (County Road 41). The parking area for Ganondagan State Historic Site is on Boughton Hill Road, near the corner of Victor-Bloomfield Road (State Route 444). N42° 57.685 - W77° 24.788
Alternative Parking:	Fishers Firehall on the south side of High Street, Victor (0.25 mile south of Valentown Museum). N43° 1.225 - W77° 25.994
Hiking Time:	3 hours one way
Length:	5.8 miles one way
Difficulty:	🥾 🥾 🥾
Surface:	Mowed-grass and dirt trail
Trail Markings:	Red blazes and diamond-shaped, red metal markers
Uses:	🚶
Dogs:	OK
Contact:	Victor Hiking Trails 85 East Main Street, Victor, NY 14564-1397 (585) 234-8226 message line www.victorhikingtrails.org

This trail is steeped in history and is a wonder of diverse terrain. The journey begins at Ganondagan State Historic Site, once the home of a thriving seventeenth-century Seneca Indian village. Its downfall came in 1687 when the Marquis de Denonville, Governor General of New France, led an army of 3,000 men from Canada to massacre the Seneca in an effort to eliminate them as competitors in the international fur trade business.

In 1998 a replica Seneca bark longhouse was built on the site using red cedar, white cedar, and hickory. It was built with intimate attention to detail using information from oral, archaeological, and historical records. The interior is furnished with hundreds of reproduced Seneca and

European artifacts from 300 years ago to help interpret the history of the fur trade in the late 1600s and the relationship between the Seneca and the European colonists. The village at Ganondagan is thought to have had more than 150 longhouses, housing as many as 4,500 people. Each longhouse housed up to 20 families. Hours that the longhouse is open for viewing vary throughout the year. Call (585) 924-5848 for the current schedule.

From Ganondagan, this trail winds through Victor, passing through Ambush Valley. In 1687 when the Marquis de Denonville and his soldiers came to Ganondagan, most of the Seneca warriors were in Illinois fighting the French. The few who remained attempted to ambush Denonville's army in this narrow valley, but they were significantly outnumbered.

The Seneca Trail traverses wooded hills, crosses shrub fields, passes through wetlands, and follows two abandoned rail lines for part of its path. One was the Rochester and Auburn Railroad. The other was an electric trolley line that connected Rochester and Canandaigua before the advent of the interstate highway system. Much of I-490 utilizes the old trolley bed. At one point along Seneca Trail, the hiker is treated to a view of the Rochester skyline in the distance.

Trail Directions
- From the parking area head north through the opening in the split-rail fence to cross a mowed-grass area toward a sign "Trail of Peace." You are following the Earth is Our Mother Trail for the first segment. See a detailed map on page 82.
- Pass the longhouse. Head into the woods behind it, passing the silver and black "Ethnobotanical Trail" sign.
- Follow the purple marked trail until it meets the red-blazed Seneca Trail.
- Follow the red trail east to Victor-Bloomfield Road.
- Turn left along the road to cross a driveway then head back into the woods.
- Cross Dryer Road (at 1.3 miles) and pass through an RG&E substation.
- The trail follows the abandoned Auburn rail line (white blazed) and crosses School Street and Rawson Road.
- Watch for a right turn off the railbed. The red-blazed trail will loop past historic village artifacts (also known as a dump).
- Watch for a trail to the left. Turn left (W). (Straight leads to Route 96).
- Pass abandoned metal and brick buildings on your right.
- Cross several bridges and boardwalks while passing through a wetland area.

- A right turn onto a straight segment of trail puts you on the abandoned trolley bed. (If leaves are off the trees, you can see the Auburn Trail running parallel to the left.)
- Turn right and cross a wooden bridge. (Left connects to the Auburn Trail, straight is the continuation of the Trolley Trail.)
- Cross a boardwalk then three wooden bridges.
- Emerge from the woods and cross a small wooden bridge.
- Turn left onto the driveway of Auburn Creek Golf.
- At Route 251, turn right.
- Cross Route 96, looking for the red marker on a post. You've come 3.7 miles.
- Follow the washed-out old dirt road uphill, bearing left.
- Part way up the hill, turn left (NW) off the road. Cross a small stream.
- Pass conglomerate rocks, cross a farm road, and continue straight through a field.
- Enter Ambush Valley (lined with horsetail plants). Watch for poison ivy.
- Cross a gravel road and enter woods.
- Emerge from the woods and turn left (N) parallel to the Thruway.
- At Willowbrook Road, turn right (E) and walk through two road tunnels under the New York State Thruway.
- After the metal gates on the left, turn left at the green and yellow "Hiking Trail" sign and climb the hill.
- Bear right at a junction.
- Continue straight (N) through two mowed-grass trail intersections.
- Climb a long, gradual hill to a view of the Rochester skyline.
- Then a long downhill along the edge of the woods.
- Bear right as a small trail heads left.
- Climb steps and turn right along the edge of a yard.
- At the gravel road, turn right and cross grass to the firehall parking lot.

Date Hiked: _____

Notes:

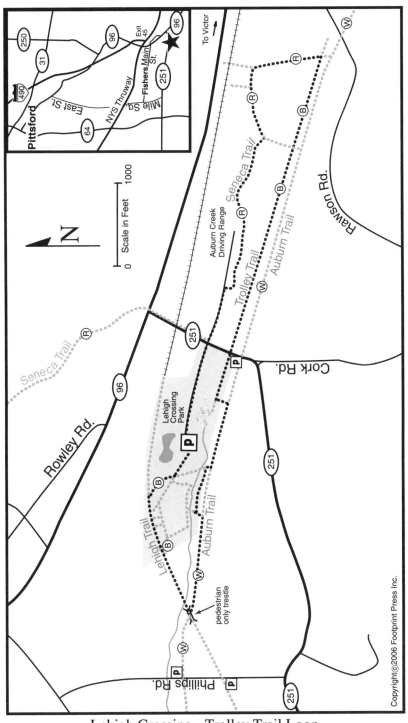

Lehigh Crossing - Trolley Trail Loop

19.

Lehigh Crossing - Trolley Trail Loop

Location: Victor, Ontario County
Directions: From Route 96 in Victor, turn west on Route 251.
                  Cross over railroad tracks, then turn right into Lehigh
                  Crossing Park. Drive back and park near the pond (no
                  official parking area has been built yet).
                  N42° 59.808 - W77° 26.368
Alternative Parking: A 2-car parking area along Route 251, next to the
                  Auburn Trail. N42° 59xxx - W77° 26xxx
Hiking Time: 2.5 hour loop
Length: 4.3-mile loop
Difficulty: 👣 👣

Surface: Mowed-grass, dirt, and hard-packed crushed stone
Trail Markings: Red blazes and diamond-shaped, red metal markers
Uses: 🚶 🎿

Dogs: OK
Contact: Victor Hiking Trails
                  85 East Main Street, Victor, NY 14564-1397
                  (585) 234-8226 message line
                  www.victorhikingtrails.org

                  Town of Victor, Parks & Recreation
                  85 East Main Street, Victor, NY 14564-1397
                  www.victorny.org/parks

From Lehigh Crossing Park you can hike several loops, depending on
how long you prefer to walk, using the Lehigh Crossing Park Trails, the
Lehigh Trail, the Auburn Trail, the Trolley Trail, and the Seneca Trail. The
terrain is flat to gently rolling hills. From 2004 through 2006 the Lehigh,
Aururn and Trolley Trails underwent major upgrading and resurfacing projects and now sport a har-packed crushed stone surface.

Look for beaver activity (dams and chewed trees) in Lehigh Crossing
Park along the feeder branch to Irondequoit Creek.

The Auburn Trail is on the bed of the Auburn and Rochester Railroad
which opened in 1840. Charles Fisher owned over 1,000 acres of land in

Beavers inhabit the Lehigh Crossing Park area.

this area and operated a sawmill. "He donated a right-of-way through his land. In exchange, he got an agreement that trains would stop at Fishers twice a day, that he would be the station agent, and that he would have the contract for supplying the railroad's lumber needs" per his great-grandson J. Sheldon Fisher in a dedication speech for this park in 2001. "Charles Fisher cleared the trees from the swampland, then abandoned the land."

The Trolley Trail is on the bed of the old Rochester and Eastern Rapid Railway, built in 1902 to run from Rochester, through Canandaigua, to Geneva. Electric trolley cars ran this route until 1930. On the segment of trails you'll walk, the Auburn Trail parallels the Trolley Trail for several miles. Back in the early 1900s, this provided the perfect opportunity for steam and electricity to see which train propulsion was faster. A race was set up with the R&E interurban trolley racing against a passenger train on the New York Central tracks. The electric trolley won and a party ensued near the cobblestone pumphouse in Fishers with a band, games, songs, refreshments, fireworks and a "shooting of the anvil." According to J. Sheldon Fisher, "a blacksmith formed a two-inch-deep trough in an anvil and filled it with gunpowder. Another anvil was placed on top of the first anvil, and a long fuse was lit to announce the arrival of the trolley in Fishers. The blast was heard over 4 miles away in Victor." Relics from the race (a photo, the motorman's hat and badge and the railroad conductors hat, badge and coat) are at Valentown Museum.

Trail Directions
- From the pond area, head west on the wide trail.
- Watch for a blue-blazed trail to the right, and turn right onto the Trolley Trail.
- Bear right at the Y to stay on the blue-blazed trail.
- Meet the ballast stone and grass Lehigh Trail, and turn left.
- Just before the trestle bridge head left down the sloped connector trail, and turn left at the base of the hill onto the white-blazed Auburn Trail.
- At the first junction, marked by a "Beaver Bridge" sign, turn left then a quick right to follow the Trolley Trail (currently marked with orange/yellow ribbons).
- When you meet the Auburn Trail again, turn left to follow it.
- Again turn left at the orange-ribboned trail, then turn right onto the blue-blazed Trolley Trail.
- Cross Route 251, and continue following the blue trail.
- At the next junction the Seneca Trail is to the left, the Auburn Trail to the right, continue straight on the red and blue trail.
- Turn left at the second red trail junction. You're now on the Seneca Trail.
- Watch for the red trail to turn left. Continue following the red trail until it reaches the driveway for Auburn Creek Golf.
- Turn left, follow the driveway, cross Route 251, and continue into Lehigh Crossing Park.

    Date Hiked: _____
    Notes:

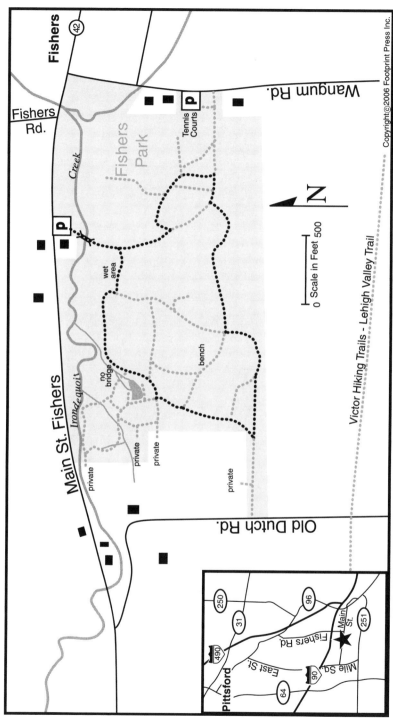

Fishers Park Trail

20.

Fishers Park Trail

Location: Fishers Park, Main Street, Fishers
Directions: From Route 96, head west on Main Street, Fishers, just south of the Thruway. The Fishers Park parking area will be on the left, past Wangum Road.
N43° 0.564 - W77° 28.417
Alternate Parking: At the tennis courts on Wangum Road
N43° 0.410 - W77° 28.226
Hiking Time: 1 hour loop
Length: 1.6-mile loop (darkened trail)
3.2 miles total trails
Difficulty:

Surface: Dirt and mowed-grass paths
Trail Markings: None
Uses:

Dogs: OK on leash
Contact: Town of Victor
85 East Main Street, Victor, NY 14564
(585) 924-7141

Victor Hiking Trails
85 East Main Street, Victor, NY 14564-1397
(585) 234-8226 www.victorhikingtrails.org

Fishers Park was part of the original Fisher homestead where pioneer Charles Fisher prospered by clearing the forest, sawing the lumber in his mills and selling the cleared land to farmers. The next generation of Fishers, brothers William and Henry Pardee Fisher, operated a nursery here, specializing in newly developed varieties of apples and pears, per William's grandson, J. Sheldon Fisher at a park dedication ceremony in 2001. The western part of the park, which is rolling grasslands today, was pasture land for cattle and sheep and still contains several fast-flowing springs.

In 1927, J. Sheldon Fisher used white-washed stones to spell out "Fishers," 110-feet-long and 10-feet-high on the hilltop to help early bi-plane pilots find their way to Rochester. Some white stones can still be found on the hill above the present day tennis courts.

The dedication ceremony, where J. Sheldon Fisher spoke, commemorated the expansion of Fishers Park. In 2001 Chauncy Young (a founding and active member of Victor Hiking Trails) sold 54 acres of land to the Town of Victor at far below market price to preserve his cherished land forever and make it available to the public. A 37.5-acre park became a 59-acre park.

Within this park, picnic tables and charcoal grills can be found at the Main Street entrance, a baseball field at the corner, and tennis courts off Wangum Road. Fisherman frequent the banks of Irondequoit Creek.

The trail described will take you across the Irondequoit Creek valley and up the facing hillside, deep within a peaceful woods. Then you'll swing west to enjoy the beautiful rolling grassland hills at the western end of the park. Sit for awhile and absorb the beauty of nature at the bench commemorating Melissa Young, Chauncy Young's daughter.

Trail Directions
- From the Fishers Park parking area, head toward the "Trail head" sign and cross Irondequoit Creek on a bridge.
- Head uphill through the woods, and take the first left.
- Take one of the trails to the right, then turn right when it ends.
- Turn left at the next junction.
- Emerge from the woods and turn left on the grassland trails.
- Take the second right on the mowed-grass trails.
- Take the third right.
- Then take the second left onto a narrow trail through a low, wet area in the woods.
- When it meets the main trail, turn left to return to the parking area.

Date Hiked: _____

Notes:

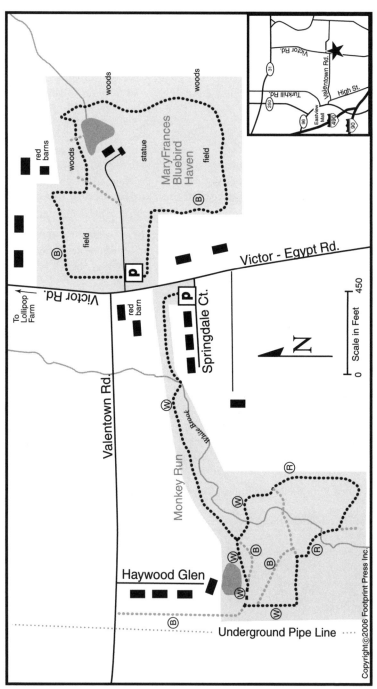

Monkey Run & MaryFrances Bluebird Haven

21.

Monkey Run

Location:	At the corner of Victor Egypt Road (County Road 9) and Springdale Court, Victor, Ontario County
Directions:	From Route 96, near Eastview Mall, turn east onto High Street and left (E) onto Valentown Road. Turn right (S) onto Victor - Egypt Road, and take the next right onto Springdale Court. Immediately turn right into the gravel parking area toward the yellow and green "Hiking Trail" sign. N43º 1.555 - W77º 24.022
Hiking Time:	45 minute loop
Length:	0.8-mile loop
Difficulty:	👣 👣
Surface:	Woodland path
Trail Markings:	Blue, white and red metal markers
Uses:	🚶 🎿
Dogs:	OK
Contact:	Victor Hiking Trails 85 East Main Street, Victor, NY 14564-1397 (585) 234-8226 message line www.victorhikingtrails.org

Valentown Road was formerly known as Monkey Run. The winding road reminded residents of a jungle vine wrapping around one tree after another, possibly providing a means of transport for an imaginary troupe of monkeys. The pond that the trail passes was known as the Black Lagoon by this property's former owners. It's home to snapping turtles.

A series of trail loops wind through the valley and hillsides of White Brook through a mature forest. White Brook is a twisting little waterway that adds a scenic dimension to this hike. The trails can be wet and muddy in early spring, but recent scout projects help keep your feet dry by providing bridges for the many brook crossings. Troop 86 scouts built 2 of the bridges. Nature signs along the way describe trees and vegetation that you pass. They were an Eagle Scout project of Zachary Rheaume from Troop 92.

Follow the trail markers to stay on the publically permissible trails. There are several side trails that lead to private homes.

Trail Directions

- From the parking area, go straight on the mowed path, past the yellow and green "Hiking Trail" sign, following the white blazes.
- At the first junction, turn right.
- The white trail will take two sharp turns.
- Turn right onto the red trail.
- Pass an unmarked trail to the right, then one to the left.
- The trail straight ahead will turn into the white trail.
- At the next junction, turn right and follow white blazes back to the parking area.

Date Hiked: _____

Notes:

22.

MaryFrances Bluebird Haven

Location:	235 Victor Egypt Road (County Road 9), Victor, Ontario County (see the map on page 100)
Directions:	From Route 96, near Eastview Mall, turn east onto High Street and left (E) onto Valentown Road. Turn right (S) onto Victor Egypt Road and pull into driveway #235 near the large green "Welcome to MaryFrances Bluebird Haven" sign. The parking area is to the right. N43° 1.629 - W77° 23.996
Hiking Time:	30 minute loop
Length:	1.1-mile loop
Difficulty:	👟👟
Surface:	Mowed meadow and woodland path
Trail Markings:	Blue blazes on wooden stakes and trees, and blue VHT markers
Uses:	🚶 🎿
Dogs:	Pets are NOT allowed
Contact:	Victor Hiking Trails 85 East Main Street, Victor, NY 14564-1397 (585) 234-8226 message line www.victorhikingtrails.org
	Town of Victor, Parks & Recreation 85 East Main Street, Victor, NY 14564-1397 www.victorny.org/parks

Welcome to the nature preserve known as the MaryFrances Bluebird Haven. This land was donated to the town of Victor in November 1996 for use as a bluebird sanctuary, by Robert Butler in memory of his wife, MaryFrances. An angel statue was added to the property at its dedication in June 1997. Watch for it as you hike. The Butler's bright blue house on the property is now used as a resource center by the Town of Victor.

The trail circumnavigates the property on a mowed path through a meadow and forest. Please follow the blue markers carefully and stay on the trail. Enjoy a quiet stroll on this forever-wild land without disturbing the nest boxes in the meadow areas. On a December afternoon hike we flushed a hawk and an owl from their perches as we hiked this trail.

Eastern bluebirds are in danger because they are cavity-nesting birds. The dead trees and wooden fence posts that once provided homes are rapidly disappearing as we convert our forests and farmlands to housing developments. Other species such as house sparrows and starlings compete with the bluebirds for the few remaining cavities. In many areas of the country, bluebird trails are being created to encourage bluebird survival. These consist of nesting boxes spaced at least 100 yards apart in fields and mowed-grass areas.

The MaryFrances Bluebird Haven is a bluebird habitat developed in support of the bluebird survival effort. This site has become an active breeding site for bluebirds and a living classroom, with an emphasis on preservation and restoration of New York's official state bird. For more information on bluebirds, visit the North American Bluebird Society web site at www.nabluebirdsociety.org.

Trail Directions
• From the parking area, head north on the mowed path, toward the "Trail Head" sign.
• Follow the well-marked blue trail around the perimeter of the field, then into the woods and back to field, to loop back to the parking area.

Date Hiked: _____

Notes:

Walks in Wayne, Seneca and Cayuga Counties

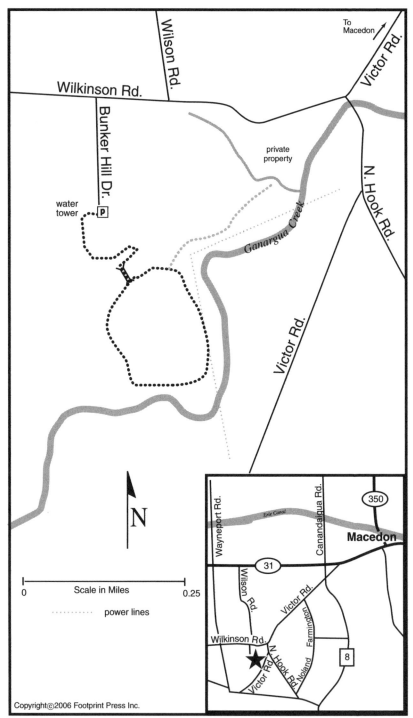

Wilson Rd.

Wilkinson Rd.

Bunker Hill Dr.

To Macedon

Victor Rd.

private property

N. Hook Rd.

water tower

P

Ganargua Creek

Victor Rd.

N

Scale in Miles

0

0.25

.... power lines

Wayneport Rd.

Erie Canal

Canandaigua Rd.

350

Macedon

31

Wilson Rd.

Victor Rd.

Farmington

Wilkinson Rd.

N. Hook Rd.

Noland

8

Ganargua Creek Meadow Preserve

23.

Ganargua Creek Meadow Preserve

Location:	Bunker Hill Drive, Macedon, Wayne County
Directions:	From Route 31, west of Macedon, head south on Wayneport Road. Turn left (E) onto Wilkinson Road, then right (S) onto Bunker Hill Drive. Drive to the end of the road, and park in spaces on the left. N43º 2.480 - W77º 20.949
Hiking Time:	30 minute loop
Length:	1-mile loop
Difficulty:	👣 👣 👣 👣
Surface:	Dirt trail down hillside then mowed field trail through the meadow
Trail Markings:	Green and white metal markers along the woods trail, none in the meadow
Uses:	🚶
Dogs:	OK on leash (please clean up after your pet)
Contact:	Genesee Land Trust
	500 East Avenue, Suite 200, Rochester, NY 14607
	(585) 256-2130 www.geneseelandtrust.org

The Ganargua Creek Meadow Preserve trail begins at the water tower, high on top of Bunker Hill. It winds down a steep hillside through an oak forest to the floodplain meadow of Ganargua Creek. Hemmed in by hills, a mowed path circles around the grassy meadow. Look for butterflies and evidence of the power of water in spring runoff as you hike the meadow, but keep an eye out for poison ivy. Go when the leaves are off the trees for the best view from Bunker Hill.

This land was donated to the Genesee Land Trust in 1996 for preservation in honor of Tim Johnson by his mother and step-father, Cynthia and Leo Kesselring. The trail was built by a class of RIT students in 2002 and is now maintained by the Macedon Trails Committee.

Trail Directions

- From the parking area, head up the hill toward the water tower. The trail begins to the left, in the woods. Follow it downhill.
- Cross the bridge at the base of the hill, and follow the perimeter trail around the meadow.
- Cross the bridge again, and head uphill to the parking area.

Date Hiked: _____

Notes:

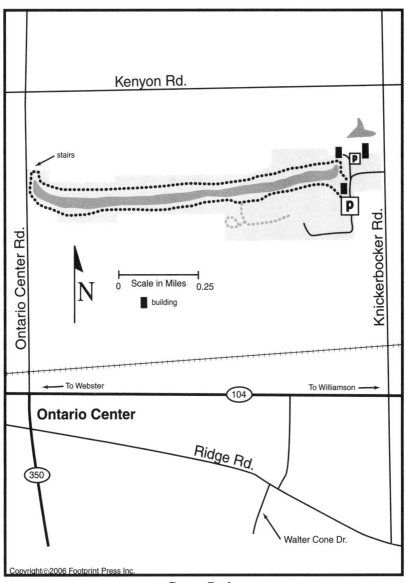

Casey Park

24.

Casey Park

Location:	Town of Ontario, Wayne County
Directions:	From Route 104 in Ontario, head north on Knickerbocker Road, and watch left in 0.5 mile for Casey Park. Within the park, bear left to find the main parking lot, past the Ontario Parks and Recreation building. N43° 14.119 - W77° 17.310
Hiking Time:	1 hour loop
Length:	1.8-mile loop
Difficulty:	🥾 🥾
Surface:	dirt trails
Trail Markings:	None
Uses:	🚶 all trails 🚴 ♿ south shore trail only
Dogs:	Pets OK on leash
Contact:	Town of Ontario Parks and Recreation Department 6551 Knickerbocker Road, Ontario, NY 14519 (315) 524-7447

The showcase of Casey Park is a long, narrow spring-fed pond around which the trail loops. The trail on the southern side of the pond is a flat, 8-foot-wide, tree-covered, packed-dirt trail that's suitable for bikes and wheelchairs as well as hikers. As the trail rounds the western tip of the pond, it narrows and climbs up steps to the top of the hill that forms the northern shore. Now the trail is a narrow woods path that weaves up and down with the contours of the terrain, offering views of the pond below.

This park owes its existence to the geology and industrial history of Ontario. Between Ridge Road (Route 104) and Lake Ontario, a layer of iron ore crops out from below a ridge of limestone. The layer of limestone and iron continue south, but as they do, the dirt and rock on top become deeper and deeper. So, it's only around Ontario that the red-colored ore, called hematite, is economical to mine. The Ontario vein was discovered in 1811 by Mr. Knickerbocker as he dug a well to water his cattle.

Mining operations soon began using horses, dump carts and a lot of manual labor. First the men hauled away the dirt to reach the ore lying

The narrow trail north of Casey Park pond.

anywhere from 10 inches to 14 feet underground. A ball drill and blasting powder were used to break the ore into manageable chunks. It was then hauled by horse cart to a pier in Bear Creek harbor and loaded onto boats for shipment to Charlotte. In early mining operations, the dirt was filled back into the hole to leave an unmared landscape.

Eventually miners had to dig deeper and deeper. By the late 1880s steamshovels and steam locomotive trains were introduced. The area was dotted with mines (Moon Bed, Bean Bed, Wayne Ore Bed, Bundy Ore Bed, Hurley Bed, etc.) and with large blast furnace smelting operations. These operations dug deep pits that eventually filled with spring water, like the pond at Casey Park. And they left long, narrow mounds of rubble like the one under the trail you'll hike north of the lake. Mining operations in the area ceased in the 1940s.

The Earl E. Casey Town Park began in 1964 with an initial purchase of 67 acres. It now encompasses 75 acres and offers a swim beach, canoe and paddle boat rental, ball fields, playground, lodge and pavilion rentals, restrooms, and trails.

Trail Directions
- From the parking area, cross the grass toward the pond and head west toward the woods, parallel to the pond.
- A few gravel trails to the left head back toward the active park area, but continue along the water's edge.
- At the end of the pond follow the water's edge around, climb a flight of stairs and head east on top of the rubble pile.
- When the trail ends, continue around the end of the pond to return to the parking area.

Date Hiked: _____
Notes:

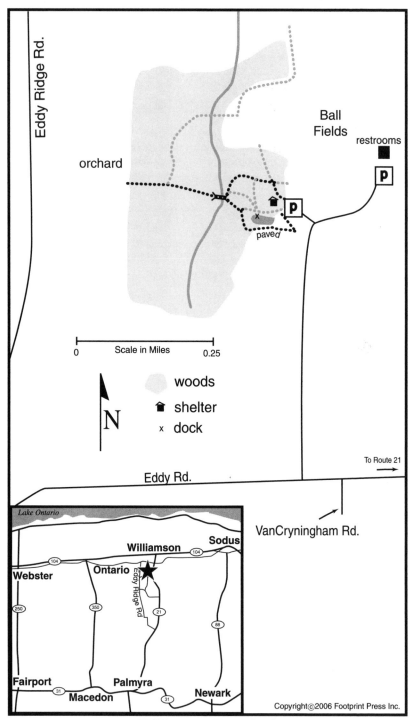

Williamson Town Park

25.

Williamson Town Park

Location:	3773 Eddy Road, Williamson, Wayne County
Directions:	From Route 104 in Williamson, head south on Route 21. Turn right (W) onto Eddy Road. In 0.4 mile turn right into Williamson Town Park. Take the first left and park by the green-roofed picnic pavilion. N43º 12.870 - W77º 12.100
Hiking Time:	30 minute loop
Length:	0.8-mile loop (darkened trail) 1.6 miles total trails
Difficulty:	👞 👞
Surface:	Dirt and gravel trails; the trail south of the small pond is paved
Trail Markings:	None
Uses:	🚶 🎿
Dogs:	Pets OK on leash
Contact:	Williamson Recreation Committee P.O. Box 152, Williamson, NY 14589
	Ed Merriett 7076 Tuckahoe Road, Williamson, New York 14589 (315) 589-9791

In 2000 this park didn't exist. It's a work in progress, being crafted by the hands of many volunteers. They built baseball and soccer fields, a playground, horseshoe pits, bocce courts, restrooms, and hiking trails. The trails wind through rolling hills in a mature forest that has been logged at times.

Trail Directions
- From the south end of the parking area, follow the paved trail around the pond.
- After the trail turns to stonedust, bear left and eventually cross a bridge over a small creek.
- Continue straight on this wide trail until it dead-ends at an orchard.

- Turn around and cross the bridge again.
- After the bridge, turn left.
- Take the third trail to the right to return to the parking area.

Date Hiked: _____

Notes:

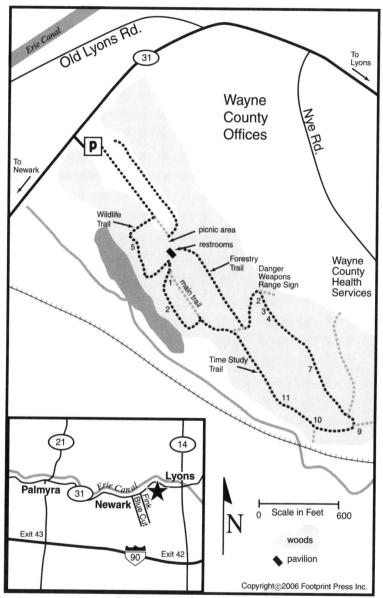

Blue Cut Nature Center

26.

Blue Cut Nature Center

Location:	Between Newark and Lyons, Wayne County
Directions:	Heading east from Newark on Route 31, Blue Cut Nature Center is on the south side of the road after Fink Road. It is marked with a large blue sign, "Blue Cut Nature Center." N 43° 3.911 - W 77° 2.291
Hiking Time:	1 hour loop
Length:	1.7-mile loop (darkened trail)
	2 miles total trail
Difficulty:	👣 👣 👣
Surface:	Dirt, mowed-grass, and pine needle trails
Trail Markings:	Trailheads are labeled with signs. Some trails have numbered, color-coded signs along the way.
Uses:	🚶
Dogs:	OK on leash
Contact:	Friends of Blue Cut
	Cornell Cooperative Extension of Wayne County
	1581 Route 88 North, Newark, NY 14513
	(315) 331-8415

The name Blue Cut dates back to 1853 when a cut was made through a drumlin while building the railroad. The Vernon Shale had a bluish cast when exposed. Today this nature center and wildlife refuge covers over forty acres.

The 1.5-mile loop described here encompasses three trails. The blue, Time Study Trail shows that everything changes, nothing is permanent. It begins in a planted 30-year-old pine forest, then climbs a drumlin formed 11,000 years ago by glaciers. The green Forestry Trail takes you through the pine plantation. The orange Wildlife Trail shows various habitats including a wetland, woods, field, and mowed-grass strips.

Trail Directions
•From the parking area, head south on the mowed-grass trail.
•Turn right onto the Wildlife Trail.

- Near the pavilion, turn right onto the main trail, then shortly turn right again toward the pond.
- At the "T" turn right onto the main trail.
- Bear right at the "Y" onto the Time Study Trail.
- Pass four trails to the right, the last one has a sign "Danger Weapons Range."
- Turn right at the next intersection.
- Near the restrooms, continue straight through a clearing, then turn right off the main trail.
- Follow this woodland trail back to the parking area.

Date Hiked: _____

Notes:

The boardwalk through Huckleberry Swamp.

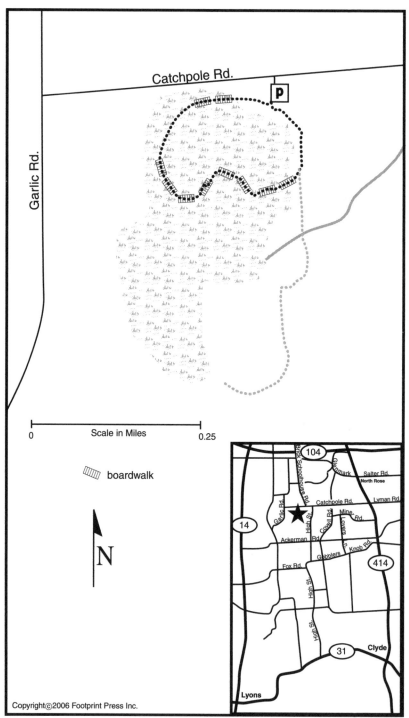

Huckleberry Swamp

27.

Huckleberry Swamp

Location:	Catchpole Road, North Rose, Wayne County
Directions:	From Route 104 (south of Sodus Bay) turn south onto Brick Schoolhouse Road. At the end, turn right onto Catchpole Road, and watch left for the entrance to Huckleberry Swamp. N43º 10.269 - W76º 56.785
Hiking Time:	30 minute loop
Length:	0.8-mile loop (darkened trail)
	1.3 miles total trails
Difficulty:	👣
Surface:	Crushed gravel and mulched trails, and extensive boardwalks
Trail Markings:	None
Uses:	🚶 ♿ (Closed from first snow until Easter.)
Dogs:	Pets NOT allowed
Contact:	Olga Fleisher Ornithological Foundation, Inc. P.O. Box 17718, Rochester, New York 14617 585) 338-1820 www.ofofinc.org

Huckleberry Swamp is 79 acres of diverse, high quality wetlands for bird and wildlife conservation. In spring, hike to the serenade of spring peepers and look for the great blue heron nests. Then return at other seasons to watch the swamp and its wildlife change.

A large, handicapped accessible, boardwalk circles through the swamp and additional trails are being built. The southern loop may even be completed by the time you visit. The trails are closed on Mondays for maintenance.

Trail Directions
• From the parking area, head toward the wooden arbor, then follow the trail on either side to hike the loop.

Date Hiked: _____

Notes:

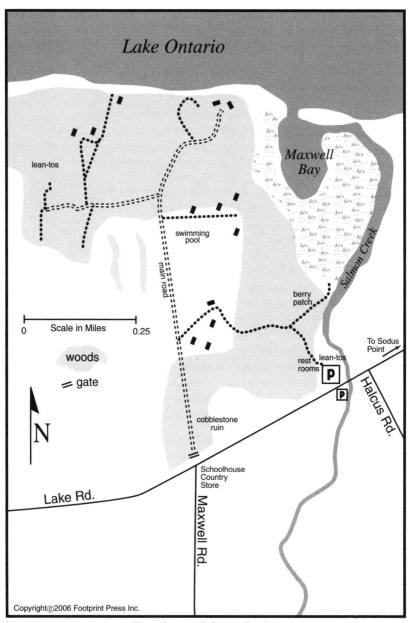

Lake Ontario

Maxwell Bay

Salmon Creek

lean-tos

swimming pool

main road

berry patch

Scale in Miles
0   0.25

woods

= gate

N

rest rooms

lean-tos

To Sodus Point

P

P

Halcus Rd.

cobblestone ruin

Schoolhouse Country Store

Lake Rd.

Maxwell Rd.

Copyright©2006 Footprint Press Inc.

Beechwood State Park

28.

Beechwood State Park

Location:	Lake Road, Sodus, Wayne County
Directions:	From Route 104 in Sodus, head north on Maple Avenue, then right (E) on Lake Road. Pass Maxwell Road then watch left for a parking area before crossing Maxwell Creek. N43º 15.911 - W77º 1.576
Alternative Parking:	Across Lake Road is another parking area. N43º 15.8653 - W77º 1.5301
Hiking Time:	30 minutes or more
Length:	1.6 miles total trails
Difficulty:	
Surface:	Abandoned gravel roads and woodland trails
Trail Markings:	None
Uses:	
Dogs:	Pets OK on leash
Contact:	NY State Office of Parks, Recreation & Historic Preservation 20th Floor, Agency Building #1, Empire State Plaza Albany, NY 12238 http://nysparks.state.ny.us

As a youngster I looked forward to my week at Girl Scout Camp Beechwood on the shore of Lake Ontario. I hiked, swam, sang goofy songs by the campfire, slept in a lean-to and generally had a grand old time. Beechwood operated as a Girl Scout camp from 1929 until New York State purchased the land in 1999 and turned it into Beechwood State Park. The park remains undeveloped, with many of the original camp structures still standing. You can wander among them on abandoned gravel roads and paths through the woods and fields.

On the property you'll find canoe/kayak access to Salmon Creek and Maxwell Bay (see *Take A Paddle - Finger Lakes New York Quiet Water for Canoes and Kayaks*), fishing access, a berry patch, Lake Ontario beach access, and ruins of an abandoned cobblestone building (see *Cobblestone Quest - Road Tours of New York's Historic Buildings*).

Lean-tos left over from when Beechwood State Park
was Beechwood Girl Scout Camp.

Trail Directions
- From the parking area, head north on the woods path with the restrooms to your left.
- The first right leads to the berry patch and fishing access.
- When you reach buildings, bear left between the first two. This will take you to the main entrance road from the old camp.
- From here, explore at will. You could spend well over an hour exploring all the roadways and trails.

    Date Hiked: _____

    Notes:

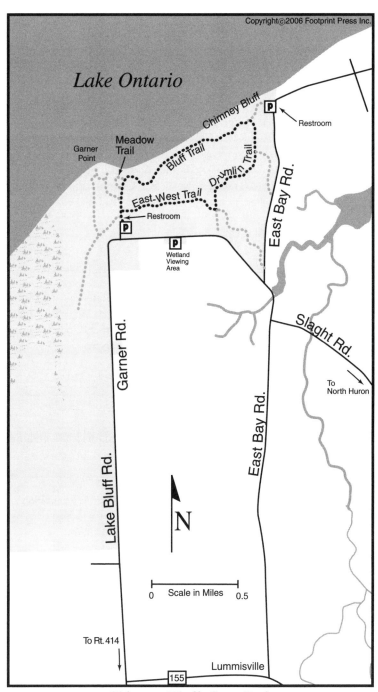

Lake Ontario

Chimney Bluff

Restroom

Garner Point

Meadow Trail

Bluff Trail

Drumlin Trail

East-West Trail

Restroom

Wetland Viewing Area

East Bay Rd.

Slaght Rd.

To North Huron

Garner Rd.

East Bay Rd.

Lake Bluff Rd.

N

0   Scale in Miles   0.5

To Rt. 414

155   Lummisville

Chimney Bluffs State Park

29.

Chimney Bluffs State Park

Location: Garner and East Bay Roads, Huron, Wayne County
Directions: From Route 104 (between Wolcott and Sodus) turn north onto Lake Bluff Road (near the northern terminus of Route 414). Continue north as it becomes Garner Road. The main entrance to Chimney Bluffs State Park will be on the left after Garner Road makes a sharp bend to the east. N43º 16.874 - W76º 55.328

Alternative Parking: At the northern end of East Bay Road. N43º 17.408 - W76º 54.390

Hiking Time: 1.5 hour loop
Length: 2.2-mile loop (darkened trail)
Other Distances: Parking lot to parking lot via the Bluff Trail - 1.3 miles
The paved Meadow Trail loop to Lake Ontario - 0.2 mile
The darkened loop + the loop to Garner Point - 3.0 miles
Difficulty: 👣 👣 West of Garner Road parking area

👣 👣 👣 👣 East of Garner Road parking area

Surface: Mowed grass and dirt trails. One short paved trail.
Trail Markings: None
Uses: 🚶 🏂 (snowmobiles on the southernmost trail only)

Dogs: OK on leash
Contact: NYS Office of Parks, Recreation & Historic Preservation
Finger Lakes Region
PO Box 1055, Trumansburg, NY 14886
(607) 387-7041 http://nysparks.state.ny.us
(315) 594-6770 local park office

Chimney Bluffs is a glacial drumlin cut to sharp spires, 150-feet-high, by wind and wave action. Drumlins are long, narrow, rounded hills of sediment (sand, clay, silt, gravel, cobbles and boulders), formed when the glaciers scoured the countryside. The last glacier to cover this area, melted 12,000 years ago. The drumlin at Chimney Bluffs has a high clay content that acts as a cement, binding gravel and cobblestones together. Still, the

The spires along Lake Ontario at Chimney Bluffs State Park.

cliff face continues to erode, as much as 5 feet per year in places, making the cliff edge trail dramatic but dangerous.

The drumlin field of which Chimney Bluffs is a part, is one of the most extensive in the world, with over 10,000 drumlins. These ridges sit north-south across this region and resemble an old-fashioned washboard.

The glaciers that sat on this land long ago pushed it downward. As the ice melted, the land rebounded. It is still rising at a rate of about a foot each century.

Several hikes are possible here. The western half of the park has mowed grass trails through fields and scrubland. The eastern half is wooded with 6 to 8-foot-wide forest trails. The bluffs face Lake Ontario with a narrow dirt trail along their edge. The highest point of land is in the northeast part of the park. The Meadow Trail is paved. The East-West Trail is part of the snowmobile trail system.

- The most popular hike is to park at either end, climb the drumlin, and hike along the top of the bluff. Depending on how far you hike before turning around, it's about a 2-mile round trip and takes about 1.5 hours.
- A loop from Garner Road toward Lake Ontario, along the Bluff Trail, south on the Drumlin Trail, then west on the East-West Trail is 2.2 miles and takes about 1.5 hours.

- A full loop leaves Garner Road heading southwest then follows the mowed grass trail north to Garner Point. From here, head east along the Bluff Trail then south on the Drumlin Trail, then west on the East-west Trail is 3 miles and takes about 2 hours.
- Or stick to a stroll on the paved Meadow Trail for a .04-mile round trip.

Date Hiked: _____

Notes:

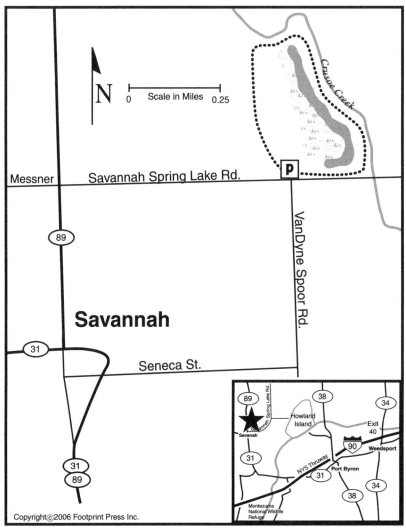

Malone's Creekside Trail

30.

Malone's Creekside Trail

Location:	Savannah Spring Lake Road, Savannah, Wayne County
Directions:	From Route 31 in Savannah, head north on Route 89. Turn right (E) onto Savannah Spring Lake Road and watch left in 0.6 mile for the parking area, marked by a large brown sign "Northern Montezuma Wetlands Project - Malone Unit #1." N43º 04.427 - W76º 44.837
Hiking Time:	25 minute loop
Length:	1.25-mile loop
Difficulty:	👢👢
Surface:	Sporadically mowed, 30-foot-wide grass path
Trail Markings:	None
Uses:	🚶 🎿
Dogs:	Pets OK on leash
Contact:	Montezuma National Wildlife Refuge
	3395 Route 5 & 20 East, Seneca Falls, NY 13148
	(315) 568-5987 www.fws.gov/R5mnwr
	New York State DEC Wildlife
	1385 Morgan Road, Savannah, NY 13146
	(315) 365-2134 www.dec.state.ny.us/website/dfwmr

This short, easy trail takes you through a mature wooded wetland then follows the top of a dike between Crusoe Creek and a pond amidst a wetland. It's mostly open to the sun, so wear a sun hat or sun lotion. Since this is a wetland, bug spray can be helpful also. Bring your binoculars - this is prime birdwatching land. As we walked, we flushed great blue herons from the creek and watched them spread their wide wings and gracefully fly away. Another heron sat perched on a post in the pond, patiently watching for fish.

Trail Directions
- From the parking area, head north (away from the road) on the wide grass path.

- Follow the path through woods, then as it bends east on a dike, passing between Crusoe Creek and a pond.
- The path will bend again to parallel Savannah Spring Lake Road and return to the parking area.

Date Hiked: _____

Notes:

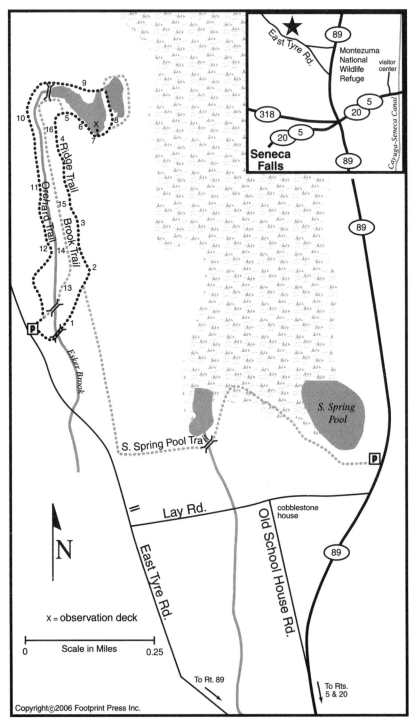

Esker Brook Trail

31.

Esker Brook Nature Trail

Location:	Montezuma National Wildlife Refuge, at the north end of Cayuga Lake, (5 miles east of Seneca Falls), Seneca County
Directions:	From Route 5 & 20, turn north on Route 89, then turn west on East Tyre Road. A gravel parking area is on the right side of East Tyre Road, 1.2-miles north of Route 89, near a large brown and white sign, "Esker Brook Nature Trail, Montezuma National Wildlife Refuge." N44° 58.438 - W76° 47.044

Alternative Parking: The South Spring Pool parking area on Route 89. N42° 58.2402 - W76° 46.2782

Hiking Time:	45 minute loop
Length:	1.5 mile loop (darkened trail)
	South Spring Pool Trail - 0.8 mile
Difficulty:	👣 👣
Surface:	Dirt and mowed-grass paths
Trail Markings:	Signs at intersections
Uses:	🚶
Dogs:	OK on leash
Contact:	Montezuma National Wildlife Refuge
	395 Routes 5 and 20 East, Seneca Falls, NY 13148
	(315) 568-5987 www.fws.gov/r5mnwr

Montezuma National Wildlife Refuge serves as a major resting and breeding area for water birds as they migrate in the spring and fall. It is situated in one of the most active flight lanes in the Atlantic Flyway.

The glaciers that scoured this area some 10,000 years ago dug the Finger Lakes and left shallow, marshy areas at the ends of the lakes. Construction of a dam at the northern end of Cayuga Lake and building of the New York State Barge Canal caused major changes to the once extensive marshes of Montezuma. By the early 1900s, all but a small portion had been drained. In 1937 the Bureau of Biological Survey, which later became the U.S. Fish and Wildlife Service, bought 6,432 acres of the former marsh. The Civilian Conservation Corps began work on a series of low dikes to hold water and restore parts of the marsh.

Today, water levels are carefully manipulated in the refuge's 3,500 acres of diked pools, to ensure that migrating birds will find suitable food and nesting habitat. In 1976 Montezuma began participating in a bald eagle release program. Over four years, 23 eagles were released and have since used Montezuma to successfully rear their young.

So why is a marsh in upstate New York called Montezuma? In the early 1800s Dr. Peter Clark, a physician from New York City, came to the area because of the salt deposits recently discovered under the marshes. He built a 12-room home (a mansion in those times) on a drumlin with a view of the marshes. Dr. Clark had traveled extensively and named his estate Montezuma in honor of the last Aztec emperor and the large marshes that surrounded Mexico City.

While at Montezuma National Wildlife Refuge for your hike, be sure to check out the other attractions. A visitor center is located off Routes 5 and 20, west of the Cayuga Seneca Canal. It is packed with exhibits and well worth a stop. From a spotting scope on the roof, you're likely to see nesting eagles and ospreys. This is also the start of the 3.5-mile wildlife drive. A brochure available at the visitor center details the sights along the way.

Spring migration of waterfowl occurs from late February through April, when 85,000 Canada geese, 12,000 snow geese, and many species of ducks use Montezuma as their northbound resting spot. Best viewing times are early morning and late afternoon. Warblers migrate in mid-May and can best be viewed from Esker Brook Nature Trail from dawn until mid-morning. April through June is wildflower season. Watch for violets, trilliums, mayapples, vetches, and mustards along the trail.

Summer is the time for waterfowl nesting. Broods of Canada geese and ducks begin to appear in early May. Great blue herons nest in the flooded timber area of Tschache Pool. Late July is peak season for the blooms of purple loosestrife, iris, mallow, and white water lily.

Fall begins the southern migration. From mid-September until freeze-up, 50,000 Canada geese and 150,000 ducks pass through the area. For shorebirds and wading birds, peak migration is mid-September. Again, they're best viewed in early morning or late afternoon.

The trails around Esker Brook are easy-to-follow dirt trails that are open for hiking only, from January through October. They're well maintained and well marked with signs. This is a wetland area, so it may be wise to

Rest at this bench overlooking the pond along Esker Brook Nature Trail.

wear bug repellent. All three trails lead through abandoned apple orchards to two man-made ponds.

The esker you'll walk was formed when a river flowed under the glacier in an icy tunnel. Rocky material accumulated on the tunnel beds, and when the glacier melted, a ridge of rubble remained.

In summer you'll see purple loosestrife along edges of the wetland, including Esker Brook Pond. This is a non-native, aggressive pest plant. It has been spreading through northern New York State rapidly. Although pretty to look at, it pushes out native plants.

A new trail has been added in recent years. The South Spring Pool Trail (0.8-mile-long) connects Ridge Trail to the Route 89 parking area.

While in the area, view the cobblestone house on Old Schoolhouse Road near the corner of Lay Road. To learn about this pre-Civil-War home construction method that was unique to this area, pick up a copy of *Cobblestone Quest - Road Tours of New York's Historic Buildings*.

Interpretive Signs Found Along The Trails:

#1. Black Walnut Trees: This native hardwood tree has long been coveted for furniture, gunstocks and veneers. To ward away nut-steelers, red squirrels chatter away at the first sign of intruders. Don't worry; they're harmless, just big talkers.

#2. The Tail Tells The Tale: If you're lucky you might catch a glimpse of a red fox, gray fox, or coyote. These are shy creatures that disappear as soon as they see, smell, or hear humans. Fur colors for all three can vary greatly. Size and position of the tail is a better

133

identifier. If you see a medium sized dog running with its tail held down between its legs, it's a coyote. Foxes are smaller and hold their tails straight out when running. The tail of a red fox is white tipped. The nocturnal gray fox has a black tipped tail.

#3. Deer Trails: Notice the worn paths on the sides of the trail that lead through thick brush? These are deer trails, made as the deer move from one feeding area to another. The white cedar trees are a favorite deer food.

#4. Living On The Edge: The zone where two or more habitats converge is referred to as an ecotone or edge. It provides a richer, more diverse attraction for wildlife. Much of the Ridge Trail is dominated by shrubs such as buckthorn and honeysuckle. Here, the shrub zone is sandwiched between the grassland and woodland.

#5. Grassland Management: Unlike most of the trails that are shaded by trees and shrubs, this area is dominated by soft-stemmed plants that provide grassland habitat. This ecological niche is inhabited by many species of insects, birds, and mammals and the species that prey on them. To counteract the natural process of succession, which would lead to the development of a young forest, this grassland is managed with mowing and controlled burning.

#6. Ecological Disaster: The shallow zones and banks of the ponds are being invaded by purple loosestrife, an exotic species of Eurasian origin. With no natural predators and extreme adaptability, this plant has quickly become a menace to the natural balance of North American wetland habitats as it outcompetes native plant species such as cattail and sedges.

#7. Wood Duck: The wood duck is easily recognized by its distinctive shape and colorful markings. The scientific name means "a waterflowl in wedding dress." The wood duck nests in tree cavities and in man-made nest boxes such as this one. There was a dramatic decline in this species at the turn of the century caused by unregulated hunting and habitat loss. Now, approximately 700 ducklings hatch each year in Montezuma's 120 nest boxes.

#8. Tree Swallows: These birds dominate the skies over the ponds much of the year with their white underparts and dark metallic blue backs. They are insectivores, flying over the grasslands and ponds, feeding on the wing. Their nests are built in tree cavities, made of grasses lined with feathers.

#9. Apple Orchard: The apple is not a particularly long-lived species, especially in the wild, so it is understandable that this remnant orchard has seen better days. Planted many years ago by farmers, the fruit now provides fall and winter food for many birds and mammals.

#10. American Beech: Smooth gray bark is the hallmark of the American beech tree. This trait has led to considerable vandalism as people carve initials in its bark. The nuts are crucial to the diets of flying squirrels, wild turkeys, ruffed grouse and others.

#11. There Is A Lot Of Life In This Dead Tree: Over time, fungi, bacteria, and invertebrates such as bristletails, wood lice, millipedes, ants, termites, and beetles will decompose this fallen tree and return its nutrients to the soil. In the meantime, this old log will provide shelter or hiding cover, denning and nesting sites, a source of food and a place to store food. Snakes, rabbits, salamanders, chipmunks, skunks, deer mice, and raccoons are just some of the species that take advantage of the habitat provided by decaying trees.

#12. Black Cherry And Shagbark Hickory: Both of these trees have unique, rough bark. The bark of the black cherry is often referred to as "potato chip" or "burnt cornflakes." In contrast, the shagbark hickory has stripes of plated bark peeling from the trunk.

#13. Snags: This rotting tree or snag is an insect smorgasbord for woodpeckers and other insectavores. Woodpeckers create cavities which become the homes of chickadees, house wrens, bluebirds, tufted titmice, and downy woodpeckers.

#14. Snakes: Docile garter snakes are frequently found sunning themselves in the narrow belt of sunlight that falls from the canopy. These small, striped snakes feed on frogs, toads, and earthworms.

#15. Understory: Buckthorn, tartarian honeysuckle, poison ivy, virginia creeper, wild grape, coralberry, and dogwood are the dominant understory species along Esker Brook.

#16. The Roots Of It All: The soil under your feet is composed mainly of glacial till, clay and organic material. The glaciers that swept through left deposits of inorganic rock, sand, and clay. As it weathered it added nutrients to the newborn soil. Clay traps the moisture and nutrients. As plants grow, die and decompose, organic material is added to the mix. Early farmers recognized the benefits of this mixture and used it extensively for decades. Now, allowed to grow wild, the lush growth of plants has quickly covered over man's influence.

Trail Directions

•Head south into the woods from the parking area on the Ridge Trail. There will be a brown and yellow sign on a post saying "Ridge Trail."

- Cross a wooden bridge over Esker Brook.
- Pass the South Spring Pool Trail to the right.
- Reach a "T." Turn right (E) toward the pond.
- Follow the mowed area close to the pond.
- Bear left around the end of the pond, then walk between two ponds.
- Reach a junction. (Left goes to Brook Trail, which returns to the parking lot on the east side of Esker Brook.) Continue straight on Orchard Trail.
- At the junction with Brook Trail, bear right to return to the parking area.

Date Hiked: _____

Notes:

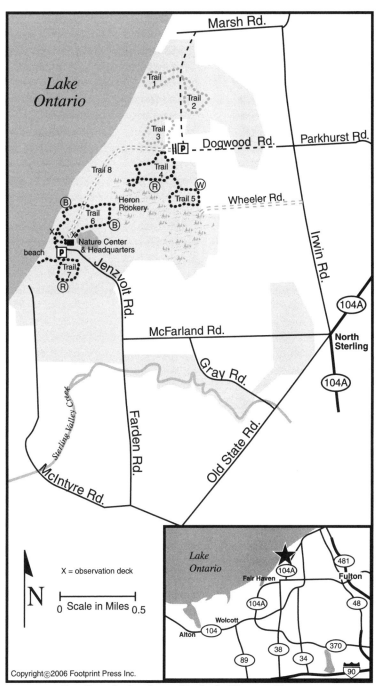

Sterling Lakeshore Park & Nature Center

32.

Sterling Lakeshore Park & Nature Center

Location:	North Sterling, Cayuga County
Directions:	From Route 104A head west on McFarland Road, then north on Jenzvolt Road to the nature center parking area. N43° 22.7009 - W76° 39.4548

Alternative Parking: At the end of Dogwood Road, in front of the Trail 8 gate. N43° 23.185 - W76° 38.575

Length:	16 miles of trails
Difficulty:	or for Trails 1,2,3 and 5
Uses:	🏃 🎿 Trail 8 only: ♿
Dogs:	OK
Admission:	Free (donation appreciated)
Contact:	Sterling Nature Center
	PO Box 216, Sterling, NY 13156
	(315) 947-6143 www.cayuganet.org/sterlingpark/

This spectacular 1,400-acre site, with nearly two miles of Lake Ontario shoreline, features glacially sculpted bluffs with scenic vistas of Lake Ontario. The land consists of a series of drumlins with intervening lowlands. The trails wind through a varied terrain of wetlands, vernal ponds, woodland, creeks, and meadows. This is a fairly new park and, as such, is a work in progress. We found some trails weren't maintained, so they're excluded from the map (#9,10, 11). Each trail is described below. We recommend the Trail 6 (0.7-mile loop) hike to visit the heron rookery or the longer (1.5-mile) Trail 4 and 5 combined loop.

The nature center is open 9 AM-3 PM weekdays and 12 PM-3 PM on the weekends. The trails are available any time. From the nature center parking area a trail leads down to the cobblestone beach, a popular summer swimming area.

There is a canoe launch in Sterling Lakeshore Park for launching into Sterling Creek. See *Take A Paddle - Finger Lakes New York Quiet Water for Canoes and Kayaks*.

Trail 1

Length:	0.7-mile loop
Hiking Time:	30 minute loop
Surface:	Woods trail
Trail Markings:	None

Trail 1 provides access to the Lake Ontario shoreline. Part of this trail traverses a young woodlot covering the nose of a drumlin. This is a good birdwatching location in spring and fall.

Trail 2

Length:	0.7-mile loop
Hiking Time:	30 minute loop
Surface:	Woods trail, sporadically maintained
Trail Markings:	None

Trail 2 traverses a wooded drumlin, once farmland and pasture, with evidence of past use. A spur visits a 50-acre beaver flow.

Trail 3

Length:	0.7-mile loop
Hiking Time:	30 minute loop
Surface:	Woods trail, sporadically maintained
Trail Markings:	None

Trail 3 is a woodland loop.

Trail 4

Length:	0.7-mile loop
Hiking Time:	30 minute loop
Surface:	A 3-foot swath mowed through the woods
Trail Markings:	Trail # sign at start, red dots on trees

Follow this pleasant loop through the woods. In spring look for the dozens of small vernal ponds. Combine it with Trail 5 for a 1.5-mile loop hike.

Trail 5

Length:	0.7-mile loop
Hiking Time:	30 minute loop
Surface:	Woods path
Trail Markings:	Trail # sign at junction with Trail 4, white triangles on trees

Accessible only from Trail 4, this loop crosses an abandoned farm site with orchards, evergreen plantations, and now forested crop fields.

Trail 6

Length:	0.7-mile loop
Hiking Time:	30 minute loop
Surface:	Woods path
Trail Markings:	Blue blazes

Follow this loop through a wildflower garden, then through woods. One observation deck overlooks Lake Ontario, another provides a view of a pond and grassland area. Be sure to take the short side trail to view the great blue heron rookery. It was loaded with nests and birds when we visited in late June.

Trail 7

Length:	0.6-mile loop
Hiking Time:	30 minute loop
Surface:	Woods trail
Trail Markings:	Green wooden arrows, red dots on trees

The Forest Ecology Trail is a loop off the nature center parking lot that features forest management exhibits. There are overlooks to a wetland and the Lake Ontario shoreline and a path leading to the beach.

Trail 8

Length:	0.5-mile linear trail
Hiking Time:	30 minutes round trip
Surface:	Double track, abandoned road (Dogwood Extension)
Trail Markings:	Trail # sign at start

Trail 8 begins behind the nature center house at a sign "no vehicles beyond this point" and leads through a small orchard. It is wheelchair accessible.

Date Hiked: _____

Notes:

Walks in Onondaga, Cayuga and Cortland Counties

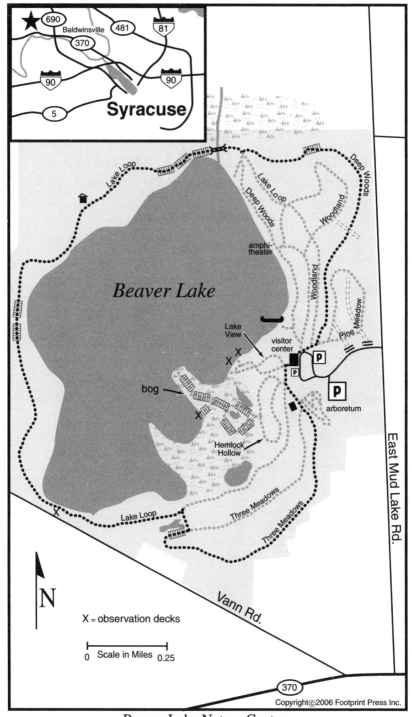

Beaver Lake Nature Center

33.

Beaver Lake Nature Center

Location:	West of Baldwinsville (20 miles northwest of Syracuse), Onondaga County
Directions:	From Route 370 (west off Route 690), turn north on East Mud Lake Road. The Nature Center entrance is on the west side of East Mud Lake Road. N43° 10.843 - W76° 24.102
Hiking Time:	2 hour loop
Length:	3.7 mile loop
	9.1 miles total trails
Difficulty:	👣 or 👣 👣
Surface:	Dirt and mulch trails and boardwalks
Trail Markings:	Wooden signs over each trailhead
Uses:	🚶 Lakeview Trail: ♿
Dogs:	Pets NOT allowed
Admission:	$2 per vehicle entrance fee
Contact:	Beaver Lake Nature Center
	8477 East Mud Lake Road, Baldwinsville, NY 13027
	(315) 638-2519
	http://onondagacountyparks.com/parks/beaver/

Beaver Lake Nature Center is a 650-acre natural community of pond, swamp, and woodland. The glacially formed lake offers a haven for thousands of migrating Canada geese in the spring and fall. Wood ducks and barred owls nest in the surrounding hardwood forest.

There are eight loop trails available to hike. The path described below follows the outer loop and takes in parts of three trails: Deep Woods Trail, Lake Loop Trail, and Three Meadows Trail. Or choose your own route, shortening or lengthening your stay to suit your energy level and time available. All the trails are easy-to-follow and well marked, so wander with peace of mind and savor the natural surroundings.

Lakeview Trail

Length:	0.3-mile figure eight loop
Hiking Time:	20 minute loop

Difficulty:

Uses:

Lakeview Trail leads to the shore of Beaver Lake. This trail is wheelchair accessible and is lined with interpretive signs which provide an introduction to this forest and lake community. On the shore is an observation platform with a telescope for wildlife observation.

Hemlock Hollow Trail
Length: 0.4-mile loop
Hiking Time: 30 minute loop
Difficulty:

Bog Trail
Length: 0.6-mile loop
Hiking Time: 40 minute loop

Hemlock Hollow Trail loops through a cool, shaded hemlock forest. A side trip from Hemlock Hollow is the 0.6-mile Bog Trail. Traverse the bog on a fern-lined boardwalk to an observation tower with a telescope. A raised platform overlooks the lily-covered pond. Along the way you can marvel at the pitcher plants and lady slipper orchids which are unique to bog environments.

Three Meadows Trail
Length: 1.5-mile loop
Hiking Time: 1 hour loop

Enjoy a sunny stroll. You'll descend into a quarried basin, a seasonal wetland reclaimed by shrubby growth and populated by a variety of songbirds and a plethora of wildflowers.

Woodland Trail
Length: 1.1-mile loop
Hiking Time: 55 minute loop

A pine forest, cedar/hemlock swamp, and a northern hardwood forest are the three different woodland communities you'll find along the Woodland Trail.

Deep Woods Loop
Length: 1.4-mile loop
Hiking Time: 1 hour loop

Hike through the serenity of a maturing forest. A boardwalk takes you safely through a wet area with sensitive and cinnamon fern. Visit the observation blind on the shore of Beaver Lake.

Lake Loop Trail
Length: 3.0-mile loop
Hiking Time: 2 hours

See the lake from every angle along the Lake Loop. Over 0.75 mile of boardwalk lets you march through a wetland without getting your feet wet.

Pine Meadow Trail
Length: 0.5-mile loop
Hiking Time: 30 minutes

Take a loop hike around this isolated meadow.

Arboretum
Length: 0.3-mile series of loops
Hiking Time: 20 minutes
Difficulty:

Follow mowed-grass paths through this young arboretum where the trees are labeled.

With a diverse aquatic environment, the Beaver Lake Nature Center is home to seven species of frogs. The tiny spring peepers are only one inch

The welcome sign for Beaver Lake Nature Center.

long but make themselves known with deafening "peeps" as they breed in April. These tree frogs have disks on their toes for climbing trees and a readily recognizable dark "X" mark on their backs. Gray tree frogs are twice the size of spring peepers. They reside in tall trees and sing with a birdlike trill for two seconds. Leopard frogs like the grassy areas of the nature center. You'll find wood frogs on the forest floor with long legs and a dark, raccoon-like mask over their eyes. Wood frogs come out at night to hunt insects and worms, then retreat beneath the leaf litter of the forest floor to escape the heat of day. In the water you'll find green frogs and bullfrogs. Green frogs grow to four inches long and sound like plucked banjo strings. Bullfrogs grow twice as large and bellow a deep "Jug-o-rum, Jug-o-rum."

Beaver Lake Nature Center also has seven species of snakes, none of them poisonous. Among them are garter snakes, ribbon snakes, northern water snakes, and milk snakes. Chances are if you see a snake, it will be a garter snake. Their name derives from the stripes along their bodies which resemble the fancy garters gentlemen used to wear to support their socks. Ribbon snakes resemble the garters but are more slender and seldom wander far from water. The northern water snake is dark-colored, thick bodied, and can grow up to 30 inches long. Brightly colored milk snakes are less common, but are distinctive with their red or copper blotches on a tan or gray background. The name derives from dairy farmers who blamed the snake for low milk production. Rather than steal milk, this snake was in the barns hunting rodents. Their stomachs can only hold a few tablespoons of liquid.

The Beaver Lake Nature Center is open year round (except Christmas Day) from 7:30 AM to dusk. In addition to nine miles of well-tended and marked hiking trails, the center offers summer canoeing, guided outings with naturalists, and exhibits.

Trail Directions
- From the visitor center, head north toward the large over-head sign for Deep Woods Trail.
- Cross a short boardwalk.
- At the trail junction, turn right on the Lake Loop Trail.
- Walk the boardwalk for about 10 minutes, traversing a swamp area with lush growth.
- When the boardwalk ends, the trail will be a six-foot-wide mulched path. Continue on the wide trail, past a trail to the right.
- A second trail to the right leads to a lean-to shelter.
- A trail to the left heads down to water's edge.

- Follow the arrow sign, and bear left at a junction with a service road.
- Pass the halfway sign. You've come 1.6 miles.
- Cross another boardwalk for about two minutes.
- Cross a bridge.
- An observation platform with a scope will be on the right, accessible from Vann Road.
- Cross a driveway.
- At the next trail junction, turn right onto Three Meadows Trail.
- A small pond is on your right.
- Turn right again at the "T."
- Cross a small boardwalk.
- You may miss the cool cover of the woods canopy if the sun is out.
- The arboretum will be on the right.
- Pass a pavilion on the left as you approach the parking area and visitor center.

Date Hiked: _____

Notes:

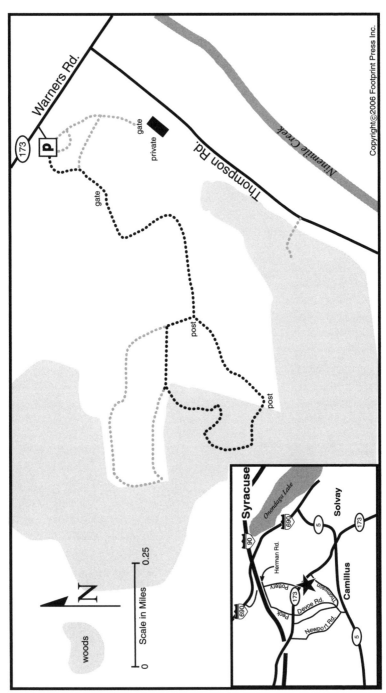

Camillus Forest Unique Area

34.

Camillus Forest Unique Area

Location:	8 miles west of Syracuse, Onondaga County
Directions:	From N.Y.S. Thruway exit 39, head south on Herman Road and Pottery Road to Route 173. Take Route 173 (Warners Road) south. Watch right (west side of Route 173) for a brown and yellow DEC sign. Follow the dirt road uphill to a parking area. N43º 4.351 - W76º 16.820
Hiking Time:	1 hour loop
Length:	2-mile loop (darkened trails) 3.1 miles total trails
Difficulty:	👣 👣 👣
Surface:	Mowed tractor path and dirt trails
Trail Markings:	2-inch round yellow plastic "Foot Trail Markers"
Uses:	🚶 🎿
Dogs:	Pets NOT allowed
Contact:	N.Y.S. Department of Environmental Conservation 1285 Fisher Avenue, Cortland, NY 13045-1090 (607) 753-3095 www.dec.state.ny.us

DEC calls this a unique area, and it is truly unique and special. It comprises 145 acres of open fields, 135 acres of early successional trees and shrubs, 38 acres of old forest, 18 acres of mature sugar maple, American beech, and bitternut hickory, and 13 acres of riparian zone. The trail follows a long, gradual uphill tractor path through fields to a stand of nearly old growth forest. Although old, this forest is not undisturbed pre-settlement "old growth" forest. The stand was harvested in the distant past, and may have been managed as a sugar bush for maple sap production. However, given the dignity of time, this forest will give us a glimpse of the transition from "old forest" to "old growth forest."

Within the old forest are several very large sugar maples, New York State's official tree. American beech can be found with diameters at breast height exceeding 36 inches. Estimated age of eleven of the dominant trees in the forest is between 120 and 200 years, with one 42-inch sugar maple tree approaching 300 years of age.

Sarah and John Vacher originally settled this land in 1796. In 1810 the Hopkins family acquired the property and continued to farm the area until the late 1880s. Agricultural statistics from 1855 describe the land as cropland, pasture, and meadow. Crops grown included potatoes, winter wheat, oats, corn, and barley. Sheep, swine, and milking cows were the dominant livestock. The 1821 Camillus census indicates that sheep significantly outnumbered other livestock, and the town produced immense quantities of wool. The Erie Canal, which opened in 1825, provided transportation for grains and wool.

Camillus Forest Unique Area was purchased by New York State in 1926. It was administered by the Syracuse Developmental Center until March 1997 when Governor George E. Pataki transferred stewardship to the DEC.

Within the old forest, wooden posts with angled tops mark points of interest. Here is the description for each post, as provided by DEC:

#1. Edge of the old forest: Congratulations! You have reached the old forest portion of the unique area. The large trees you see are sugar maple, with an occasional bitternut hickory or basswood. Sugar maple is valued for many reasons. It provides shade, sap for maple syrup, den and nesting cavities for wildlife, gives us beautiful fall color, as well as wood for flooring, furniture, and bowling pins. Like all trees, sugar maple produces oxygen, removes carbon dioxide from the environment, filters dust and absorbs noise; its roots help stabilize soils, thereby reducing sedimentation and enhancing water quality. Sugar maple requires fertile, moist soil conditions for optimum growth. It is not suited to stressful environments and is not salt tolerant, thereby making it a poor choice for planting in urban areas or along major highways.

#2. Old grader, early 1900s: This old grader was horse-drawn and probably utilized to construct farm roads. Look at plants on the ground; you will find maple leaved waterleaf, eastern waterleaf, and touch-me-not in great quantities along with occasional rock piles created by settlers clearing the land.

#3. Old stump: The cutting of this tree provided light to the forest floor and opportunities for shade-tolerant sugar maple saplings to become established in the forest understory. The trees one to two inches in diameter are nearly 40 years old. This is because they are heavily shaded, and are growing very slowly. Sugar maple has the

A horse-drawn grader sits in Camillus Forest.

ability to increase in growth once additional light is made available. Look at the forest floor, you will find Christmas ferns and blue cohosh, a plant that is an indicator of rich, limestone-based soils. You will also note a slippery or red elm, with sprouts coming from the trunk. These sprouts suggest that the tree is in decline and lacking vigor.

#4. Small natural forest opening: You have just passed through the only section of forest that has black cherry, a relatively fast-growing, shade-intolerant (light-loving) tree that belongs to the rose family. Black cherry is readily identifiable by its cornflake-like rough-textured black bark. It requires openings greater than a half acre in size to become established. This stop illustrates a natural forest opening that was created when a sugar maple and bitternut were blown down by wind. Seedlings and saplings are taking advantage of light, heat, and nutrients provided by this opening. Herbaceous and woody vegetation provides valuable browse for white-tailed deer. Red elderberry, wild leek, and American basswood can be found. Openings or lateral gaps in the canopy are typically found in forests that are developing into old growth. Spring wildflowers found in the forest include Dutchman's breeches, toothwort, purple trillium, white trillium, false Solomon's seal, yellow forest violet, and Carolina spring beauty. Initial plant surveys found nearly 80 different plants in this forest.

151

#5. Large natural forest opening: Along this segment of trail you will see a significant forest opening in the process of development. Look up at the sky and across the opening; you will see large gaps between trees and standing dead (snag) trees, some of which provide dens and cavities for wildlife such as raccoon, gray squirrel, saw-whet owl, screech owl, pileated woodpecker, and yellow shafted flicker. Insects associated with snags also provide food for wildlife. Take a minute to look and listen. You will likely hear the call of wood thrush, veery, yellow-shafted flicker, or blue jay. Birds that migrate from the tropics (neotropical migrants) such as the scarlet tanager have been observed in this forest opening as well.

#6. Decaying tree: As you walk through the forest you will find remnants of old trees, referred to by foresters as coarse woody debris. Once a tree dies, it decays and nutrients are recycled back into the soil. Here you see a tree that fell over between 10 and 15 years ago. As you walk through the forest, notice other trees that have tipped over along with portions of their root systems. As old trees tip over and decay, hummocks are created on the forest floor by the soil piles left, creating the hummock and hollow "micro topography" found in older forests. Soils in this forest are classified as chiefly Camillus, Ontario, and Hilton loams, soils that have a high natural limestone, red sandstone, and shale. These soils are very productive from a forestry standpoint. Even so, most tree roots are no deeper than 24 to 36 inches, as the roots need to exchange oxygen and carbon dioxide. Find a recently blown over tree along the trail; see how small the root system is on these large trees.

#7. Largest sugar maple trees: You are entering the portion of the forest with the largest number of giant sugar maple trees. Next to you is a 38-inch sugar maple that sheep or cattle may have once grazed around. It was a common practice for farmers to allow grazing in the forest as it prevented the forest understory from growing, thereby keeping the forest "park-like" and making activities such as firewood cutting or sugar maple sap collection easier.

#8. Largest sugar maple: This sugar maple is the largest and oldest in the forest, with an estimated age of 295 years (approximately birth date of 1712) and height of 110 feet. Maximum tree heights approach 126 feet in the forest. Note the shaggy bark, an indication of how old this tree is. Over its entire life, this tree has grown at an approximate rate of 14 rings to the inch. The average growth of young to moderately aged healthy sugar maples that are codominant to dominant in the forest canopy in Central New York is 10 rings to the inch, or two inches in a decade.

#9. Old broken American beech: American beech produces beech-nuts (hard mast) for wildlife such as the blue jay, turkey, and deer. Unfortunately, Central New York beech is dying due to beech bark scale complex, a fungus disease that eventually girdles and kills the tree. Butternut canker has killed the majority of trees in this forest stand as well. Analysis of trees over six inches in diameter shows that 83% of the forest is sugar maple and 13% is American beech. Most of the American beech will die within the next 20 to 30 years due to age and disease, providing opportunities for a new generation of trees.

#10. Exit the woods: Feel the change in temperature (depending on the season) as you exit the "big woods." On a clear day you see well into neighboring Oswego, Madison, and Oneida counties to the Tug Hill Plateau and Mohawk River valley. Look for songbirds, butterflies, turkey, deer, and an occasional coyote as you wind back to the trailhead.

Trail Directions
- From the parking area, head toward the wooden sign on a post with a round yellow trail marker.
- Follow a hedgerow, then pass through a yellow gate.
- The trail winds through fields and heads uphill. (Markers will be sporadic through this section.)
- Reach a "T" marked by a wooden post (N43° 4.110 - W76° 17.455) and turn right.
- Pass a trail to the right.
- Enter the woods. Follow the yellow markers carefully through the woods. Many other paths intersect.
- Exit the woods near another post (N43° 3.923 - W76° 17.501). Spectacular valley views await you. Notice Oneida Lake in the distance.
- Reach the trail junction and turn right (E), heading downhill all the way to the parking area.

Date Hiked: _____

Notes:

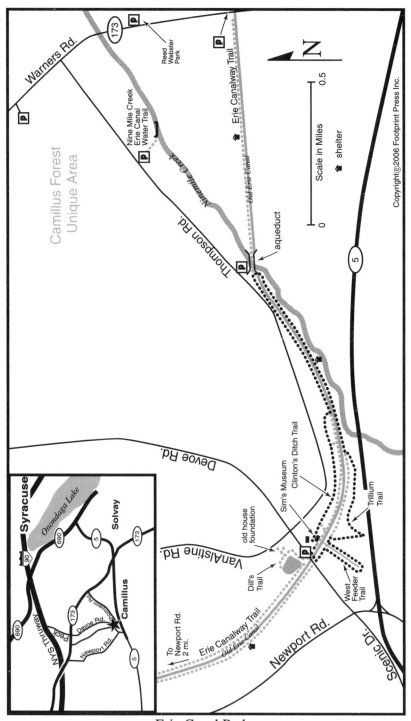

Erie Canal Park

35.

Erie Canal Park

Location:	Camillus (west of Syracuse), Onondaga County
Directions:	From Route 5, exit north onto Newport Road, then turn right onto Devoe Road. Erie Canal Park is on the right, just north of the Old Erie Canal. N43° 3.149 - W76° 18.202
Alternative Parking:	A parking area off Thompson Road, near the dock and aqueduct. N43° 4.351 - W76° 16.820
Hiking Time:	1.5 hour loop
Length:	2.5-mile loop
	3.6 miles total trails
Difficulty:	👣 👣
Surface:	Dirt and gravel trail
Trail Markings:	None
Uses:	🚶 🎿 Bikes are allowed on Erie 🚴 Canalway Trail (not on Clinton's Ditch, Trillium, or Dill's Trails)
Dogs:	OK on leash
Contact:	Erie Canal Park
	5750 Devoe Road, Camillus, NY 13031
	(315) 488-3409 http://eriecanalcamillus.com/

The enlarged Erie Canal was abandoned in 1922, then sat idle until 1972 when the town of Camillus purchased a seven-mile stretch. Since then an army of volunteers has been busy clearing the land, building dams, refilling the canal with water, and building a replica of Sims' store. The original Sims' store was built in 1856 at the intersection of Warners Road and the canal. It served as a general store, home for the Sims family, and departure point for people boarding the canal boats. The store was destroyed by fire in 1863, the replica lives on today. The first floor is setup like the original store. The second floor houses exhibits and antiques of the era along with models of locks, aqueducts, and canal boats. Sims' Museum is open Saturdays year-round from 9 AM until 1 PM, and Sundays from 1 PM until 5 PM, May through October, and 1 PM to 4 PM, November through April.

The trails are available year-round during daylight hours. This trail circumnavigates the historic enlarged Erie Canal and parallels sections of the original Clinton's Ditch. It also takes you to view the remains of the aqueduct, which once carried the canal waters over Nine Mile Creek. Volunteers at Erie Canal Park have plans to re-line the aqueduct and float water in this segment of the Old Erie Canal. Rain shelters are built at several locations along the trail.

To extend your walk, there is an additional 0.5 mile loop from the Sims' Museum on Dill's Trail. Dill's Landing was once a wide waters and boat slip along Clinton's Ditch. Cross Devoe Road, and take a quick right onto the trail. The trail will "Y" with the left leading to a view of the pond and the right leading past interpretive signs to the stone-lined cavity of the old boat slip and an old house foundation.

Trail Directions
•From the parking area at Sims' store, walk west toward Devoe Road. Just before the road, turn left and cross a wooden bridge.
•Turn left (E) onto the path on the opposite side of the canal.
•At the pedestrian bridge, turn right on the West Feeder Trail.
•Reach the end of the feeder, and turn left around its end to return on the opposite side.
•Reach the canal and turn right (E).
•Reach the entrance to Trillium Trail, and turn right.
•Cross three wooden bridges as this trail winds through the woods.
•At 0.9 mile, you'll reach the canal again. Turn right.
•Reach the dock at 1.6 miles. (A parking area is to the left on Thompson Road.) Continue straight to a dead end at the aqueduct. All that remains are the stone supports for the wooden trough and the towpath.
•Turn around and walk back to the dock.
•Turn right, then a quick left, to continue walking on the other side of the canal, now heading west.
•Turn right onto Clinton's Ditch Trail.
•Continue on the trail to the parking area at Sims' Museum.

Date Hiked: _____
Notes:

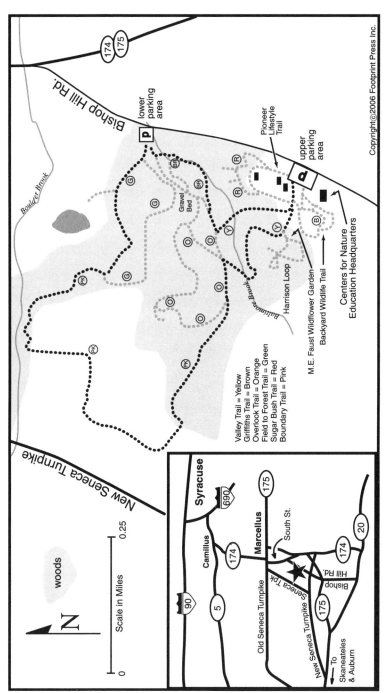

174 175

Bishop Hill Rd.

lower parking area

P

Boulder Brook

New Seneca Turnpike

woods

N

Scale in Miles

0   0.25

Pioneer Lifestyle Trail

upper parking area

Gravel Bed

G

G

G

BR

BR

R

R

O

O

O

O

Y

Y

B

PK

PK

PK

G

Baltimore Brook

Harrison Loop

M.E. Faust Wildflower Garden

Backyard Wildlife Trail

Centers for Nature
Education Headquarters

Valley Trail = Yellow
Griffiths Trail = Brown
Overlook Trail = Orange
Field to Forest Trail = Green
Sugar Bush Trail = Red
Boundary Trail = Pink

Copyright©2006 Footprint Press Inc.

Syracuse

Camillus

Marcellus

90

5

690

174

175

South St.

20

174

175

Bishop Hill Rd.

Old Seneca Turnpike

New Seneca Turnpike

Seneca Tpk

To
Skaneateles
& Auburn

Baltimore Woods

36.

Baltimore Woods

Location:	Northeast of Skaneateles Lake in the town of Marcellus, Onondaga County
Directions:	From Skaneateles, take Route 20 east, then Route 175 east. Turn left (N) on Bishop Hill Road. The upper parking area for Baltimore Woods will be on the left (W) at the top of the hill. N42° 57.920 - W76° 20.643
Alternative Parking:	Lower parking area also on Bishop Hill Road N42° 58.184 - W76° 20.544
Hiking Time:	1.75 hour loop
Length:	2.5-mile loop 5 miles total trails
Difficulty:	👞 👞 👞 Easier hikes are available.
Surface:	Wood-chipped and dirt trails
Trail Markings:	Color-coded signposts and some plastic and wooden markers, and paint blazes
Uses:	🚶 ♿ (Blue trail only)
Dogs:	Pets NOT allowed
Admission:	A $2 per person or $3 per family donation is suggested.
Contact:	Centers for Nature Education, Inc. P.O. Box 133, 4007 Bishop Hill Road Marcellus, NY 13108-0133 (315) 673-1350 www.takeahike.org

Eight loop trails cover this 170-acre nature center, owned by Save the County, Inc. (a local non-profit land trust), and managed and operated by Centers for Nature Education, Inc. (a non-profit environmental education organization). Most trails are color-coded and easy-to-follow.

The route described wanders around the outside perimeter of five of the trails in the following order:

> **Yellow – Valley Trail:** A 0.6-mile loop down the glacial valley and across Baltimore Brook.
> **Orange – Overlook Trail:** A 0.7-mile hike over glacial mounds.

Pink with pileated woodpecker symbol – Perimeter Trail: A 1.1-mile traverse of rolling terrain through woods and Boulder Brook Valley.

Green – Field to Forest Trail: A 0.75-mile traverse of rolling terrain through woods and fields. The mature forest was once a sugarbush.

Brown – Griffiths Trail: An easy 0.35-mile meanders through the active flood plain of Baltimore Brook.

Four easy trails near the parking area are not included in the route described below. They are:

Blue – Backyard Wildlife Trail: A 0.3-mile loop on level ground that winds through plantings for wildlife and is handicapped accessible.

Green signs on posts – Pioneer Lifestyle Trail: A 0.3-mile loop encircling the pioneer homestead area.

Mildred E. Faust Wildflower Garden: An easy 0.3-mile maze through labeled plantings of native wildflowers and ferns.

Harrison Loop: A 0.25-mile, easy to follow trail lined by tree trunks, that enters the wooded area surrounding Faust Garden.

Red – Sugar Bush Trail: A short loop off the Pioneer Lifestyle Trail with overlooks to the valley below.

Trail Directions

•From the upper parking area, walk behind the pavilion on a wood-chipped trail, heading toward the yellow trail.

•Pass labeled flowerbeds and continue straight.

•Enter the woods and head down hill on the yellow trail to the valley bottom.

•Cross Baltimore Brook on a wooden bridge.

•At the intersection, turn left (W) onto the orange trail.

•At the next intersection, bear left onto the pink trail.

•Follow the pink trail as it winds, then ends at the green trail.

•Turn left onto the green trail.

•From the parking area, take the wide trail away from Bishop Hill Road.

•At the next intersection, turn left onto the brown trail.

•Stay left on the brown trail until it ends at the orange trail.

•Turn left (W) onto the orange trail.

•At the next junction, turn left (S) onto the yellow trail and head downhill.

•Cross a bridge over Baltimore Brook.

•Climb through a notch in the hills beside a spring-fed stream.

•At a junction, turn left (SE) to return to the upper parking area.

A log cabin at Baltimore Woods.

Date Hiked: _____

Notes:

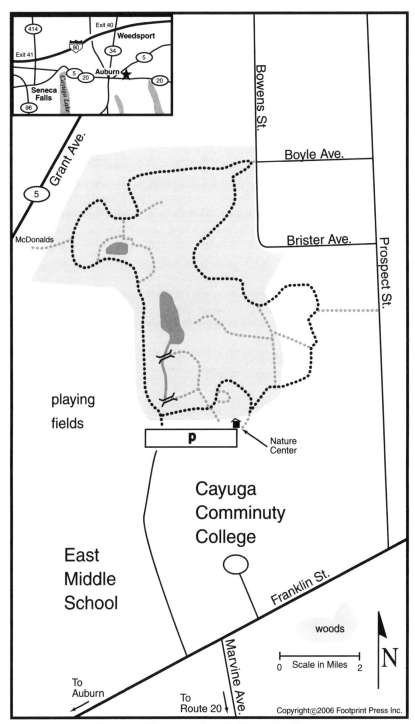

Cayuga Community College Trail

37.

Cayuga Community College Trail

Location:	Auburn, Cayuga County
Directions:	From I-90 exit 40 (Weedsport/Auburn) take Route 34 south about 8 miles into Auburn. Turn left at the first stop light inside the city limits onto Standart Avenue. Go straight through the Route 5/Grant Avenue intersection, then turn left at the next 4-way intersection onto Franklin Street. Turn left onto a driveway after East Middle School but before Cayuga Community College. Drive to a parking lot behind a white corrugated metal building. Look for a large brown sign "Cayuga Community College Nature Trail." N42° 56.727 - W76° 32.662
Hiking Time:	30 minute loop
Length:	1-mile loop
	1.5 miles total trails
Difficulty:	👟 👟
Surface:	Stonedust and mowed-grass
Trail Markings:	None
Uses:	🚶 🎿
Dogs:	OK on leash
Contact:	Cayuga Community College
	197 Franklin Street, Auburn, NY 13021
	(315) 255-1743

Here's a small natural oasis in an urban area. The man-made ponds and trails were built in 1978. Look for barbed wire fencing, rock piles and old apple trees, evidence that this land was farmed back in the 1950s. Over the years, 6,000 conifer seedlings were planted.

The main perimeter trail is stone dust. Some interior trails are mowed-grass or dirt that can be muddy. Most of the trails are flat or mildly undulating. The southweast section is more hilly.

Trail Directions

• Begin the trail at the main entrance, at the west end of the parking area.
• Stay on the 6-foot-wide stonedust trail as it winds around the perimeter of the wooded area.

Date Hiked: _____

Notes:

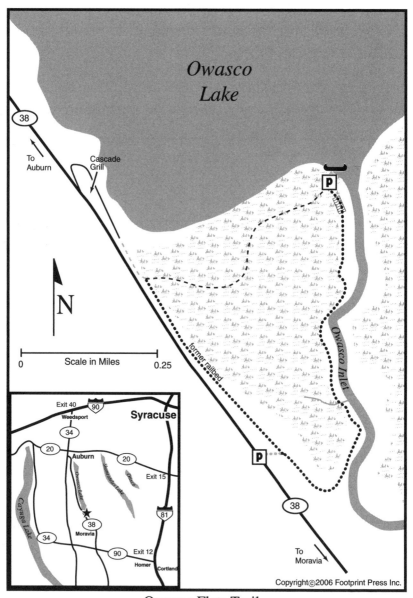

Owasco Flats Trail

38.

Owasco Flats Trail

Location:	The south end of Owasco Lake, Cayuga County
Directions:	From Route 38 at the south end of Owasco Lake, turn east on a small road toward the Cascade Grill. At the base of the hill, continue straight past two brown signs "Cayuga County Parks & Trails" onto a gravel road. Follow it to a circle at Owasco Inlet. N42º 45.291 - W76º 27.849
Alternative Parking:	A break in the guardrails along Route 38. N42º 44.876 - W76º 27.979
Hiking Time:	1 hour loop
Length:	1.6-mile loop
Difficulty:	🥾🥾
Surface:	Dirt (can be muddy)
Trail Markings:	None
Uses:	🚶
Dogs:	OK
Admission:	Free
Contact:	Cayuga County Parks & Trails Commission Emerson Park, 6914 East Lake Road, Auburn, NY 13021 (315) 253-5611 www.cayuga.ny.us/parks/

Welcome to Owasco Flats — a large fern and willow marsh, and flood plain forest with Owasco Inlet running down its middle. Owasco Flats was also the original name of the town of Moravia. This fertile valley was cultivated by the Indians. Around 1850 a plank road was built across it, later replaced by the Lehigh Valley Railroad which is now abandoned. The hiking loop will utilize the old railbed.

We first discovered this trail while looking for a take-out point when paddling Owasco Inlet for our guidebook, *Take A Paddle - Finger Lakes New York Quiet Water for Canoes and Kayaks*. When we came back to hike it, we were pleasantly surprised to find a nice loop trail. Expect to get your feet muddy, and you'd be wise to take along some bug spray.

Trail Directions

•From the parking area, head south along the inlet on a boardwalk.

•The dirt trail narrows into a woods path, still running parallel to the inlet.

•The trail will bend inland and meet the 4-foot-wide former railbed.

•A side trail leads to the alternative parking area, but continue on the rail-trail until it ends at the gravel entrance road.

•Turn right, and follow the gravel road back to the parking area.

Date Hiked: _____

Notes:

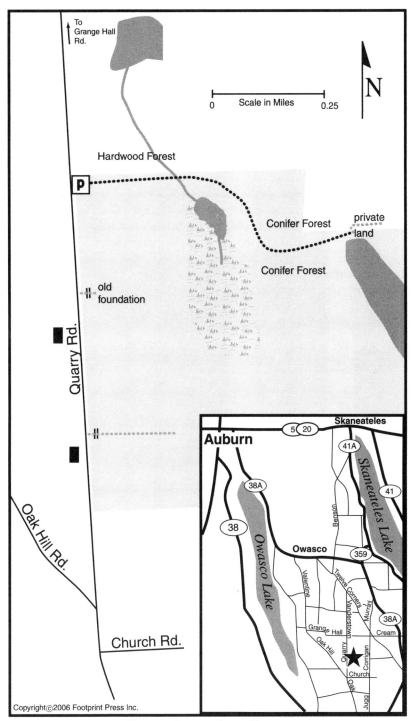

To
Grange Hall
Rd.

Scale in Miles
0   0.25

N

Hardwood Forest

P

Conifer Forest   private
                        land

old
foundation   Conifer Forest

Quarry Rd.

Oak Hill Rd.

Church Rd.

Skaneateles
5 20
41A
Auburn
38A   41
Skaneateles Lake
38   Owasco   359
Owasco
Owasco Lake
                        Benson
                        Twelve Corners
                        Valentine
                        Vanderstown
                        Murray
                        38A
                        Grange Hall   Cream
                        Oak Hill
                        Corrigan
                        Quarry
                        Church
                        Oak

Copyright©2006 Footprint Press Inc.

Frozen Ocean State Forest

39.

Frozen Ocean State Forest

Location:	Southeast of Owasco Lake, Cayuga County
Directions:	From Skaneateles take Route 41A South. Turn right onto County Route 359, then left (S) on Route 38A. Turn right on Cream Hollow Road (it turns into Grange Hall Road). After 1.2 miles, turn left onto Quarry Road. The trail head is in 0.8 mile on the left. There's room for one car at the trailhead. N42° 47.831 - W76° 25.954
Hiking Time:	1 hour
Length:	1.6 miles round trip
	0.8 mile total trails
Difficulty:	👟 👟
Surface:	Dirt
Trail Markings:	None
Uses:	🚶 🎿
Dogs:	OK
Contact:	DEC Region 7
	615 Erie Boulevard West, Syracuse, NY 13204-2400
	(315) 426-7403 www.dec.state.ny.us

This trail is for those who enjoy a route-finding challenge. The trail is along fire lanes and logging roads that are minimally maintained and unmarked, so it can be hard to follow. The DEC web site map shows a loop trail, but we were not able to locate it. We fear is has overgrown beyond recognition. Still, the path that exists is a quiet walk through a mixed hardwood forest and a conifer forest. You pass a wetland and the trail ends at a pond. It's pretty in spring with marsh marigolds, trillium, virginia waterleaf, skunk cabbage, hepatica, spring beauties, dames rocket, bloodroot, May apple, touch-me-not, wild ginger and Salomon's seal all in bloom.

The land was clear-cut and settled by Irish immigrants fleeing the potato famine in the mid-1800s. The high elevation (1,620 feet) made farming difficult, so the settlers moved on, but the foundations, wells, and plantings remain. Why it's called Frozen Ocean is a mystery. At times it has been called Slate Hill because flagstone was quarried here. New York State purchased the land for reforestation.

Trail Directions
•From the trailhead, follow the trail east.
•Cross a stream that connects two ponds.
•The hardwood forest turns into a conifer forest.
•The trail ends at the north end of a pond. (The trail with yellow dots is on private property.)
•Turn around to follow the same path back to the parking area.

Date Hiked: _____

Notes:

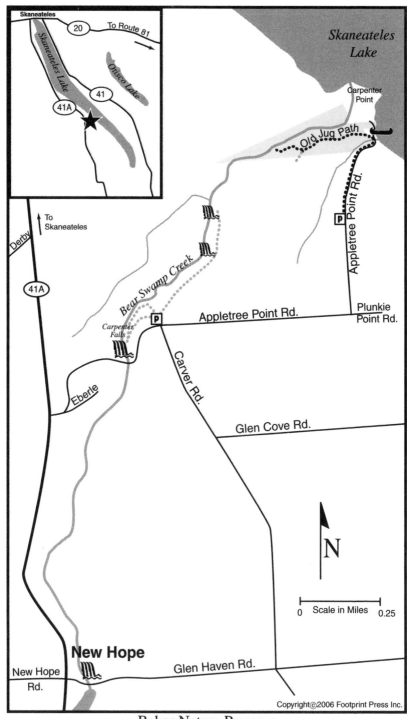

Bahar Nature Preserve

40.

Bahar Nature Preserve

Location:	The west shore of Skaneateles Lake, Cayuga County
Directions:	15 miles south of Skaneateles on Route 41A, turn east onto Appletree Point Road (there's a historical marker for Millard Fillmore's homesite at the corner). Follow Appletree Point Road as it takes a 90-degree left turn. Watch for the gravel parking area on the left. N42° 49.071 - W76° 19.821
Hiking Time:	45 minutes round trip
Length:	1.3-mile round trip
Difficulty:	👣 👣 👣
Surface:	Dirt
Trail Markings:	None
Uses:	🚶 🚶
Dogs:	OK on leash
Contact:	Finger Lakes Land Trust 202 East Court Street, Ithaca, NY 14850 (607) 275-9487 www.fllt.org

Old Jug Path is a faint old road that once led from the lake to a distillery by the waterfalls. It wanders through a mixed forest, overlooking the Bear Swamp Creek ravine. As you hike, listen for the songs of birds and the rush of water from Bear Swamp Creek.

Hu Bahar was a wilderness and nature lover who intended to keep this forested gorge untouched. Honoring her late husband's wishes, Dawn Bahar sold the 25-acre parcel at a reduced price to the Finger Lakes Land Trust in 1998. Part of Bahar Preserve includes a 65-foot crescent of Skaneateles lakeshore. Steps lead down to it from Appletree Point Road, or paddle your canoe or kayak to this spot and use the Old Jug Path to stretch your legs.

On your way driving to Bahar Nature Preserve, you passed Carpenter Falls. This waterfall and its surrounding land is a new acquisition of the Finger Lakes Land Trust. Their intent is to sell the land to New York State

DEC. The trails to it are described in *200 Waterfalls in Central and Western New York - A Finders' Guide*.

Trail Directions

•From the parking area on the west side of Appletree Point Road, walk the road heading left (N).

•Follow the road as it bends left and heads downhill.

•After a green sign, "NYS Environmental Protection Fund - Bahar Nature Preserve" (N42º 49.273 - W76º 19.715) and a small creek, turn left to begin on the trail. (The stairs to lake access will be to your right).

•Head steeply uphill. Then the trail will level out.

•At the "Y," the branch to the left dead ends at a yellow sign "Nature Preserve ends here." N42º 49.237 - W76º 19.971. The branch to the right is longer but has a steep section. It dead ends at N42º 49.247 - W76º 20.040.

•Turn around and follow the same path back to the parking area.

Date Hiked: _____

Notes:

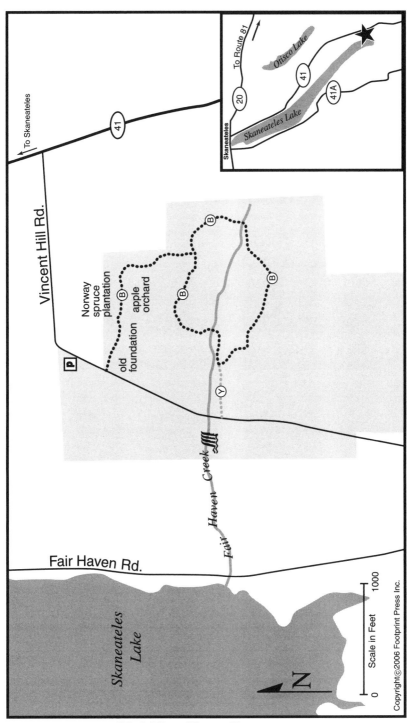

High Vista Nature Preserve

41.

High Vista Nature Preserve

Location:	Southeast of Skaneateles Lake, Town of Scott, Cortland County
Directions:	From Route 41, south of Skaneateles, turn west onto Vincent Hill Road (just north of the Cortland and Onondaga County line). After the road bends, there is a small parking area on the right. N42° 46.287 - W76° 15.629
Hiking Time:	45 minute loop
Length:	1.2 mile loop 1.5 miles total trails
Difficulty:	👣 👣 👣
Surface:	Dirt
Trail Markings:	Blue and yellow blazes
Uses:	🚶
Dogs:	OK on leash
Contact:	Finger Lakes Land Trust 202 East Court Street, Ithaca, NY 14850 (607) 275-9487 www.fllt.org

This preserve is part of the area at the south end of Skaneateles Lake, designated by the Audubon Society as an Important Bird Area, containing critical habitat for birds. Particularly at risk are the cerulean warblers that nest here.

The trails are well-marked and well-maintained. They lead through an old apple orchard and a young forest. Fair Haven Creek, which bisects the loop, is filled with many small waterfalls. The forest floor as well as tree canopy offer a sea of green. Hike when leaves are off the trees to see a view of Skaneateles Lake in the valley below.

As we hiked, we spooked a small group of deer. Also, a hawk was drinking from the spring fed stream and took flight through the forest when he spotted us. In addition to the wildlife, we enjoyed seeing jack in the pulpits and wild strawberry along the trail.

Trail Directions

- From the parking area, head south along Vincent Hill Road to the green sign "High Vista Preserve."
- Head up the trail.
- When the blue-blazed trail comes to a "T" you can follow the loop in either direction.
- Then follow the same path back to the parking area.

Date Hiked: _____

Notes:

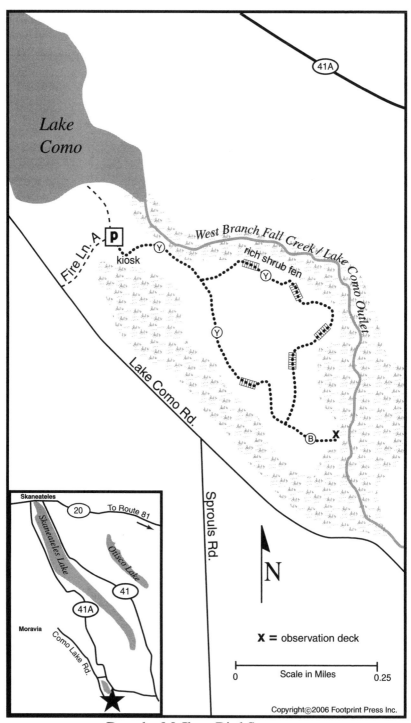

Dorothy McIlroy Bird Sanctuary

42.

Dorothy McIlroy Bird Sanctuary

Location: South of Lake Como, Summerhill, Cayuga County

Directions: From Skaneateles, take Route 41A south. Turn right onto Branch Road, north of Lake Como. Turn left onto Lake Como Road. After Lake Como, watch left for a green and white "Dorothy McIlroy Bird Sanctuary" sign and a sign with a blue "A." Turn left at the sign, onto Fire Lane A. The parking area will be on the right. N42° 40.373 - W76° 17.920

Hiking Time: 45 minute loop

Length: 1.2 mile loop (total trails)

Difficulty:

Surface: Dirt

Trail Markings: Yellow and blue blazes

Uses:

Dogs: OK on leash

Contact: Finger Lakes Land Trust
202 East Court Street, Ithaca, NY 14850
(607) 275-9487   www.fllt.org

Dorothy McIlroy, a renowned birder, was instrumental in starting the Laboratory of Ornithology at Cornell. Following her death in her 90s, her children donated money to establish a bird habitat preserve in her memory. Combined with anonymous monetary donations and the donation of a 28-acre tract by Dr. and Mrs. James Bugh of Cortland, the Dorothy McIlroy Bird Sanctuary was established and has grown to 156 acres in size.

This preserve sits at the outlet of Lake Como, along the upper reaches of Fall Creek. It's located in a pocket of high plateau with weather a bit colder than the surrounding area and is considered a boreal swamp forest. Hemlock and yellow birch grow here — trees more typical in the Adirondack Mountains. The cool temperatures and northern plant species support breeding populations of northern birds such as dark-eyed junco, hermit thrush, winter wren, Canada warbler, and mourning warbler.

A rich shrub fen in Dorothy McIlroy Bird Sanctuary.

Also, this site contains one in a chain of rich shrub fens along Fall Creek. A rich shrub fen is shrubland on woody peat that is fed by waters rich in minerals. Stop at the kiosk near the beginning of the trail to read the diagrams that differentiate a fen from a bog.

We found this walk particularly interesting. You walk on soft duff, the accumulation from a forest that has stood here many years. Look closely at the lumpy ground — evidence that it was never farmed. However, the tree hillocks and old stumps show that it was harvested for lumber. Be sure to take the blue side trail to the overlook. A viewing deck with benches overlooks the creek and surrounding wetland full of sedges, dead trees, and of course, lots of birds.

Trail Directions
•From the parking area, follow the mowed path into the woods.
•At the "T," bear right to continue on the yellow loop.
•Watch for the blue-blazed side trail to the overlook.
•Return on the blue trail, and turn right to continue on the yellow trail.
•Watch right for the unusual fen vegetation.
•Turn right to follow the yellow trail back to the parking area.

Date Hiked: _____

Notes:

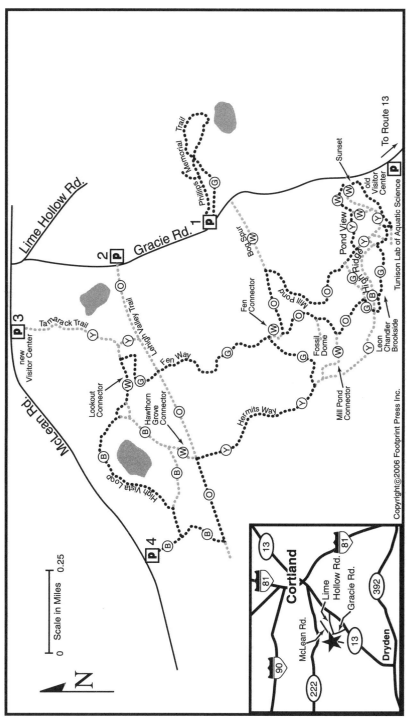

Lime Hollow Nature Center

43.

Lime Hollow Nature Center
for Environment & Culture

Location: Southwest of Cortland, Cortland County
Directions: Follow Route 13 south from Cortland. Turn north on
                         Gracie Road. Parking will be on the west side of Gracie
                         Road at the sign "Tunison Lab of Aquatic Science."
                         N42º 33.404 - W76º 14.699
Alternative Parking #1: Farther north on the east side of Gracie Road at
                         the Phillips Memorial Trailhead.
                         N42º 33.745 - W76º 14.839
Alternative Parking #2: Still farther north on the east side of Gracie Road
                         at the Lehigh Valley Trailhead.
                         N42º 33.932 - W76º 14.939
Alternative Parking #3: On the south side of McLean Road, west of Lime
                         Hollow Road, at the Tamarack Trailhead. (This is the
                         future site of the new visitor center.)
                         N42º 34.168 - W76º 15.095
Alternative Parking #4: Farther west on McLean Road, at the High Vista
                         Loop Trailhead. N42º 33.853 - W76º 15.780
Length: 7.6 miles total trails
Difficulty: Varied, see recommended hikes below
Surface: Dirt trails
Trail Markings: Color-coded markers
Uses:

Dogs: OK on leash
Contact: Lime Hollow Center for Environment & Culture
                         3091 Gracie Road, Cortland, NY 13045-9355
                         (607) 758-5462   www.limehollow.org

The Lime Hollow Center has expanded significantly since our first edition of *Take A Hike*, both in acreage and in trail miles. It now covers 375 acres of diverse woodlands with over 7 miles of trails. There is a visitor center on Gracie Road with interpretive exhibits and live animal exhibits. It also offers restrooms, a water fountain, and a picnic area. The visitor center is open Monday through Saturday from 9:00 AM to 5:00 PM and Sunday from 1:00 PM to 4:00 PM. A new visitor center is being built on McLean Road.

Fossil Dome is a unique feature of Lime Hollow Nature Center. Off Mill Pond Trail, it's a site where many fossils can be found. Another unique feature is the Tunison Lab of Aquatic Science, which is open to visitors. Salmon, rainbow, and lake trout can be seen in indoor and outdoor raceways. Or, learn about a bog by hiking the self-guided interpretive Phillips Memorial Trail.

The trails are well marked with signs coded by color:

Name	Color	Distance	Difficulty
Sunset Trail	White	0.2 mile	2 boots
Pond View Trail	Yellow	0.3 mile	2 boots
High Ridge Trail	Blue	0.2 mile	2 boots
Leon Chandler Brookside	Green	0.4 mile	1 boot
Mill Pond Connector	White	0.2 mile	3 boots
Mill Pond (Fossil Dome spur)	Orange	1.0 mile	3 boots
Bog Spur	White	0.2 mile	1 boot
Fen Connector	White	0.5 mile	2 boots
Hermits Way	Yellow	0.8 mile	2 boots
Fen Way	Green	0.6 mile	2 boots
Phillips Memorial Trail	Green	0.7 mile	1 boot
Lehigh Valley Trail	Orange	0.8 mile	1 boot
Hawthorn Grove Connector	White	0.1 mile	2 boots
High Vista Loop	Blue	1.0 mile	2 boots
Lookout Connector	White	0.3 mile	2 boots
Tamarack Trail	Yellow	0.3 mile	1 boot

Hike Recommendation #1
Hiking Time: 30 minute loop
Length: 0.7-mile loop
Difficulty:

Park at alternative parking lot #1 and hike the Phillips Memorial Trail (green), following a glacial esker to a bog.

Date Hiked: _____

Notes:

Hike Recommendation #2
Hiking Time: 1.5 hour loop
Length: 3.3-mile loop
Difficulty:

Park at alternative parking lot #4, and hike the High Vista Loop (blue), Lookout Connector (white), Fen Way (green), Hermit's Way (yellow) and Lehigh Valley Trail (orange).

Date Hiked: _____
Notes:

Hike Recommendation #3
Hiking Time: 1.5 hour loop
Length: 3.0-mile loop
Difficulty:

Park at the old visitor center on Gracie Road, and take a hilly hike following the Sunset (white), Pond View (yellow), Mill Pond (orange), and Leon Chandler Brookside (green) Trails.

Date Hiked: _____
Notes:

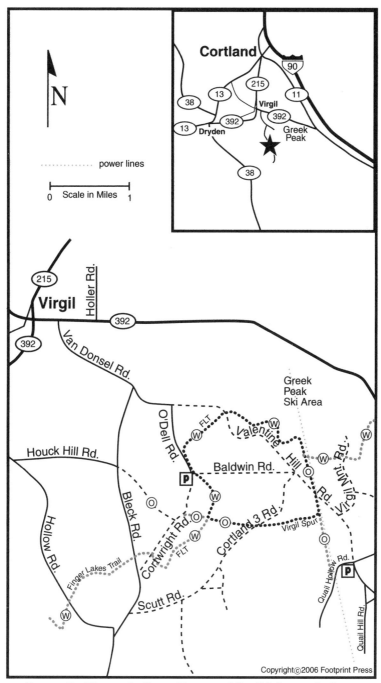

James B. Kennedy State Forest - Virgil Mountain Loop

44.

James B. Kennedy State Forest —
Virgil Mountain Loop

Location:	James B. Kennedy State Forest, Virgil, Cortland County
Directions:	From Route 392 in Virgil, turn south onto VanDonsel Road. Pass Bleck Road, and turn south onto O'Dell Road. There's room to park 1 or 2 cars across from Baldwin Road. N42° 29.239 - W76° 9.683
Hiking Time:	2.5 hour loop
Length:	4.7-mile loop
Difficulty:	👣 👣 👣 👣
Surface:	Dirt
Trail Markings:	White and orange blazes
Uses:	🚶 ⛷
Dogs:	OK on leash
Contact:	Finger Lakes Trail Conference

Finger Lakes Trail Conference
6111 Visitor Center Road, Mt. Morris, NY 14510
(585) 658-9320   www.fingerlakestrail.org

NYS Department of Environmental Conservation
1285 Fisher Avenue, Cortland, NY 13045-1090
(607) 753-3095   www.dec.state.ny.us

The Virgil Mountain Loop in James B. Kennedy State Forest uses a segment of the white-blazed Finger Lakes Trail and the orange-blazed Virgil Spur Trail to create a loop. Many of the roads in James B. Kennedy State Forest are very rough seasonal roads — often better suited to hiking than to driving. Expect a woodland hike through rugged terrain.

Trail Directions

- From the parking area, follow the white-blazed Finger Lakes Trail north along O'Dell Road, and continue following it as it veers right into the woods.
- Cross a dirt road (Valentine Hill Road). N42° 29.791 - W76° 9.142

•At the clearing under power lines, the white Finger Lakes Trail continues east. You need to head south below the power lines on the orange trail.
•Cross a dirt road (Valentine Hill Road again). N42º 29.146 - W76º 8.197
•At the next trail junction, turn right to follow the orange Virgil Spur.
•Cross a dirt road (Cortland 3 Road). N42º 28.879 - W76º 8.643
•At the next intersection, turn right onto the white Finger Lakes Trail, and follow it back to the parking area.

Date Hiked: _____

Notes:

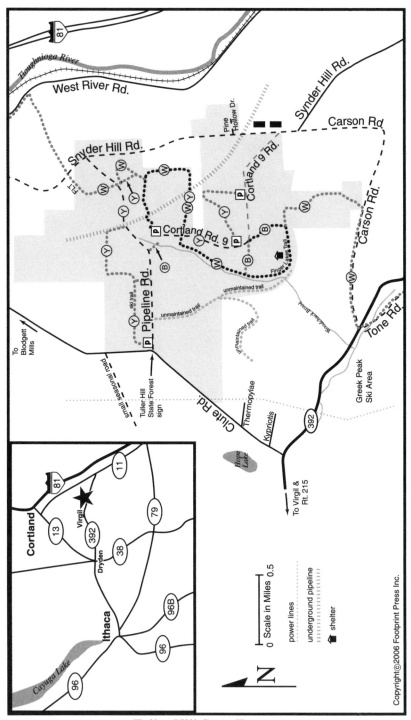

Tuller Hill State Forest

45.

Tuller Hill State Forest

Location:	Blodgett Mills, Cortland County
Directions:	From Route 392, across from Greek Peak Ski Area, turn east onto Carson Road. Notice the white blazes signifying that the Finger Lakes Trail follows this road for a while. Follow Carson Road around a sharp bend, then turn left onto Cortland 9 Road. Park in the circle at the northern end of Cortland 9 Road. N42º 31.492 - W76º 9.960
Hiking Time:	2.5 hour loop
Length:	4.4-mile loop
Difficulty:	👣 👣 👣 👣
Surface:	Dirt
Trail Markings:	White, blue and yellow blazes
Uses:	🚶
Dogs:	OK on leash
Contact:	Finger Lakes Trail Conference 6111 Visitor Center Road, Mt. Morris, NY 14510 (585) 658-9320 www.fingerlakestrail.org
	NYS Department of Environmental Conservation 1285 Fisher Avenue, Cortland, NY 13045-1090 (607) 753-3095 www.dec.state.ny.us

The roads within Tuller Hill State Forest (especially Pipeline Road and Snyder Hill Road) are all rough, dirt seasonal roads that are more suited to hiking than driving. They're hilly and shaded by an overhanging canopy of trees. The Finger Lakes Trail winds through Tuller Hill State Forest as part of its 563-mile journey across southern New York State. This white-blazed trail and its blue-blazed side trails are well-maintained and easy to follow. Also within this park are yellow-blazed and unblazed trails that are sporadically maintained and can be difficult to follow.

The recommended loop creates a figure 8 by following the Finger Lakes Trail, part of a blue-blazed side trail, and yellow-blazed Cortland 9 Road, a seasonal dirt road.

Trail Directions

- From the parking loop at the north end of Cortland 9 Road, follow the unmarked trail uphill from the northeast corner.
- At the junction, turn right and follow the white-blazed Finger Lakes Trail. It will swing back downhill, cross the underground pipeline and cross Cortland 9 Road.
- Stay on the white-blazed trail, passing a blue-blazed trail to the left and the Woodchuck Hollow lean-to.
- At the next junction, turn left onto the blue-blazed trail.
- At Cortland 9 Road turn left, and follow the road north to the parking area.

Date Hiked: _____

Notes:

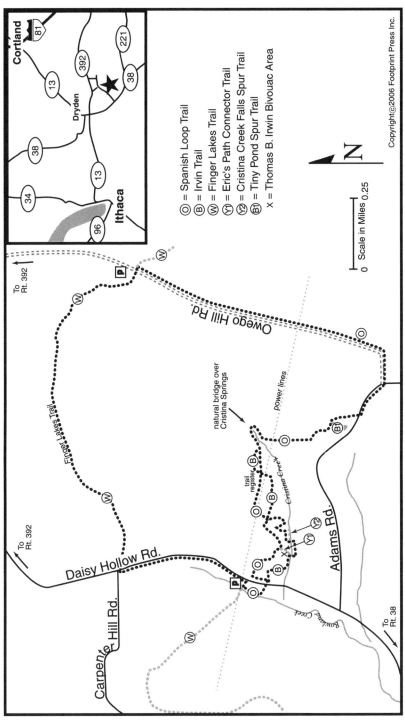

Legend

◎ = Spanish Loop Trail
Ⓑ = Irvin Trail
Ⓦ = Finger Lakes Trail
Ⓨ₁ = Eric's Path Connector Trail
Ⓨ₂ = Cristina Creek Falls Spur Trail
Ⓑ₁ = Tiny Pond Spur Trail
x = Thomas B. Irwin Bivouac Area

Copyright©2006 Footprint Press Inc.

Scale in Miles
0   0.25

N

Cortland
81
221
392
13
38
Dryden
38
13
34
96
Ithaca

To Rt. 392
P
To Rt. 392
Ⓦ
Ⓦ
Ⓦ
Finger Lakes Trail
Daisy Hollow Rd.
Carpenter Hill Rd.
Ⓦ
Owego Hill Rd.
◎
Ⓑ₁
natural bridge over Cristina Springs
power lines
trail register
Ⓑ
Ⓑ
◎
Cristina Creek
Ⓨ₂
Ⓨ₁
x
Ⓑ
◎
P
◎
Rowland Creek
Adams Rd.
To Rt. 38

Spanish & Irvin Loop Trails

46.

Spanish & Irvin Loop Trails

Location:	Dryden Lake State Multiple Use Area, Harford, Cortland County
Directions:	From Dryden, head south on Route 38. Turn left (N) onto Daisy Hollow Road. After passing Adams Road (also called Adams Hill Road), watch left for a small grass parking area. N42º 27.793 - W76º 13.941
Uses:	🚶
Dogs:	OK
Admission:	Free. Closed during big game hunting season (approximately November 15 through December 15)
Contact:	Finger Lakes Trail Conference
	6111 Visitor Center Road, Mt. Morris, NY 14510
	(585) 658-9320 www.fingerlakestrail.org
	NYS Department of Environmental Conservation
	1285 Fisher Avenue, Cortland, NY 13045-1090
	(607) 753-3095 www.dec.state.ny.us

The orange-blazed Spanish Loop Trail and the blue-blazed Irvin Trail are part of the Finger Lakes Trail System. Together with the white-blazed Finger Lakes Trail, they create short and long loop hiking options. Hiking here takes you through private property. Please stay only on the marked trails. Camping is permitted only in the bivouac area marked by a X on the map.

Spanish Loop Trail

Hiking Time:	3 hour loop
Length:	5.7-mile loop
Difficulty:	👣 👣 👣
Surface:	3.6 miles of woods trail, 1.3 miles of seasonal dirt road, 0.8 mile of paved road
Trail Markings:	White and orange blazes

The Spanish Loop Trail was added as a part of the Finger Lakes Trail System in 2003 thanks to the work of Alex and Michele Gonzales. To complete the loop requires some road walking — 0.8 mile of pavement and 1.3 miles on a sunny dirt road — but you'll also enjoy miles of woods walking with views of Daisy Hollow and Rowland Ridge. You'll pass a mossy natural bridge over Cristina Springs and cross through a magical forest with a floor covered in ferns.

Trail Directions

- From the parking lot on Daisy Hollow Road, follow the white blazed trail away from the road for 100 feet to the bank of Rowland Creek.
- Turn left and follow the orange-blazed trail.
- Cross Daisy Hollow Road and climb Adams Hill following the orange trail through a tree farm. (Pass blue and yellow trails that form the Irvin Loop — see the Irvin Trail information below.)
- Pass through a logged area. Follow the blazes carefully to stay on the trail and not a logging road.
- The final blue side trail (B1) leads 225 feet to a tiny duckweed-covered pond with bullfrog serenades. This makes a nice break spot if the bugs aren't bothersome.
- In 1.7 miles, reach Adams Road and turn left, still following orange blazes.
- In 0.2 mile, turn left onto rough dirt Owego Hill Road. Orange blazes will be missing, especially on the southern section.
- After 1.3 miles, turn left into the woods on the white-blazed Finger Lakes Trail. The forest floor is densely covered in ferns. You've covered 3.2 miles so far. (A parking area is just north of this trail crossing. N42° 28.231 - W76° 12.416)
- At 4.0 miles, cross Rowland Creek.
- In another 0.7 mile, cross a small tributary and ascend an old logging road used by ATVs.
- In 0.1 mile leave the logging road on the left and descend to the banks of a creek.
- Turn left at Daisy Hollow Road and follow it back for 0.6 mile to the parking area.

Date Hiked: _____

Notes:

Irvin Loop Trail

Hiking Time:	1 hour loop
Length:	2.0-mile loop
	0.8-mile loop if you loop back on Y1
Difficulty:	👣 👣 👣
Surface:	Dirt, woods trails
Trail Markings:	Blue and orange blazes

The Irvin Loop Trail was added as a part of the Finger Lakes Trail System in 2005. You're climbing Adams Hill, so expect a steady uphill climb. The trail crosses Cristina Creek with waterfall views in spring and returns downhill through a young forest.

Trail Directions:

• From the parking lot on Daisy Hollow Road, follow the white blazed trail away from the road for 100 feet to the bank of Rowland Creek.
• Turn left and follow the orange-blazed trail.
• Cross Daisy Hollow Road.
• Turn right onto the blue-blazed trail.
• Pass the yellow-blazed trail (Y1) on the left. (Turn left here to return to the parking area for a 0.8-mile loop.)
• Cross Cristina Creek and watch left for a small waterfall.
• Cross the creek again. (A yellow trail to the right (Y2) is a 0.1-mile spur trail to another small waterfall).
• Keep following the blue trail as it crosses the orange trail.
• When the blue trail ends at the orange trail, turn right and follow the orange trail all the way back to the parking area.

Date Hiked: _____

Notes:

Walks in Tompkins County

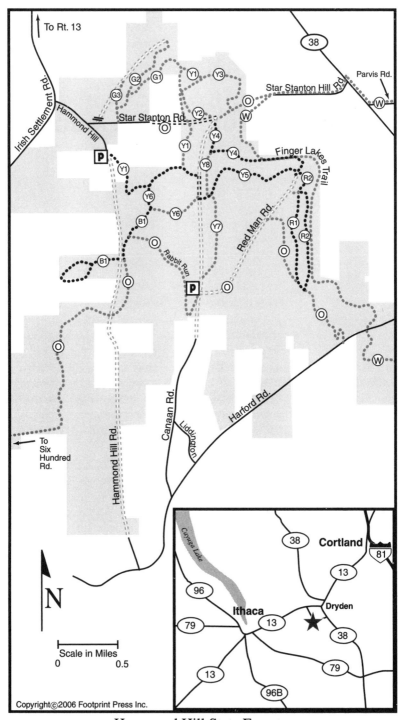

Hammond Hill State Forest

47.

Hammond Hill State Forest

Location:	Dryden and Caroline, Tompkins County
Directions:	From Ithaca, head east on Route 13. Pass Yellow Barn Hill Road, and turn south on Irish Settlement Road. Turn left (E) on Hammond Hill Road. Follow it to the end. N42° 26.211 - W76° 18.322
Length:	16 miles of trails total
Surface	Woods trails, dirt double track roads
Trail Markings:	Numbered trail junctions, round plastic markers (colored and numbered)
Uses:	🚶 🎿 🚴 🐎 🛷
Dogs:	OK
Contact:	NYS Department of Environmental Conservation 1285 Fisher Avenue, Cortland, NY 13045 (607) 753-3095 ext. 215 www.dec.state.ny.us

Hammond Hill was established as a state forest between 1935 and 1950 in an effort to reduce soil erosion, produce forest products, and provide recreational opportunities. Once depleted farmland, it was planted with thousands of pine, spruce, larch, maple, ash, cherry, and oak seedlings. Today the 3,618 acres are forested to support management activities.

Sitting above 1,800 feet in elevation, the network of trails are an active place for winter fun as well as in the other seasons. The 10.4 miles of yellow, blue, red, and green trails are for hiking, cross-country skiing, snowshoeing, mountain biking, and horseback riding. 5.6 miles of orange trails are designated for snowmobiling in winter, but allow hiking and biking the rest of the year. The white-blazed Finger Lakes Trail crosses through Hammond Hill State Forest. It is designated for hiking and snowshoeing.

Yellow Trails - 5.6 miles on old logging roads and fire lanes

Trail	Level of Difficulty	Distance
Y1	Moderate	1.9 miles
Y2	Easy	0.6 mile
Y3	Moderate (scenic view of Dryden Lake)	0.6 mile
Y4	Moderate	1.0 mile

Trail	Level of Difficulty	Distance
Y4B	Moderate	0.1 mile
Y5	Difficult	1.3 miles
Y6	Easy	0.2 mile
Y7	Difficult	1.0 mile

Blue Trail - 1.4 miles

Trail	Level of Difficulty	Distance
B1	Moderate	1.4 miles

Red Trails - 1.7 miles

Trail	Level of Difficulty	Distance
R1	Difficult	0.6 mile
R2	Difficult	1.1 miles

Green Snowmobile Trails - 5.6 miles, can be used by skiers

Trail	Level of Difficulty	Distance
G1	Difficult	0.8 mile
G2	Moderate	0.7 mile
G3	Difficult	0.2 mile

Finger Lakes Trail (white blazes)   3.2 miles

Orange Snowmobile Trail (Forest Access and Seasonal Use Roads), 5.6 miles

Recommended Hike #1: B1 Loop

Hiking Time:	1.5 hour loop
Length:	3-mile loop
Difficulty:	👢 👢 👢

Trail Directions

•From the parking area at the end of Hammond Hill Road, head southeast on Yellow Trail 1 (Y1).

•At the junction turn right onto Yellow 6.

•At the next junction turn right onto Blue 1.

•Follow Blue 1 (it will co-exist with the orange snowmobile trail for a short distance) until it loops at the end. Use it to return to Yellow 6.

•Turn left onto Yellow 6, then left again onto Yellow 1 to return to the parking area.

Date Hiked: _____

Notes:

Recommended Hike #2: Y & R Trail Loop

Hiking Time: 3.5 hour loop
Length: 6.9-mile loop
Difficulty: 👢 👢 👢 👢

Trail Directions (4 boots, 6.9 miles)
- From the parking area at the end of Hammond Hill Road, head southeast on Yellow Trail 1 (Y1).
- Pass the junction for Yellow 6, then take the next right off Yellow 1.
- Turn right onto dirt Canaan Road, then left onto Yellow 5.
- Follow Red 2 south.
- Continue south on Red 1, then return north on Red 2.
- Turn right onto Yellow 4. (It will co-exist with the white-blazed Finger Lakes Trail for a while.)
- Pass Yellow 8. The trail ends at the junction of Canaan & Star Stanton Roads (both dirt). Turn left to head west on Star Stanton Road.
- At Hammond Hill Road turn left to return to the parking area.

Date Hiked: _____

Notes:

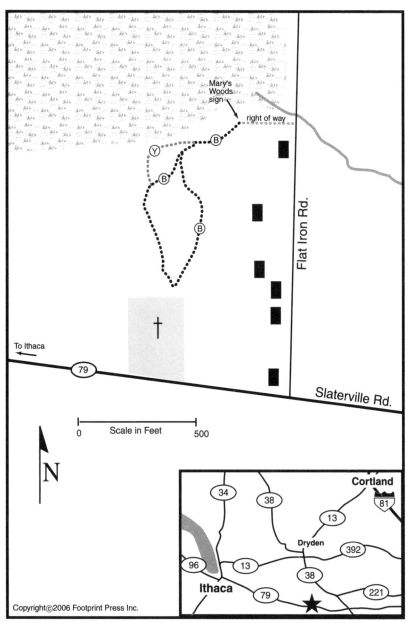

Mary's Woods sign

right of way

B

Y

B

B

Flat Iron Rd.

To Ithaca

79

Slaterville Rd.

Scale in Feet

0   500

N

Cortland

81

34

38

13

Dryden

392

96

13

Ithaca

79

38

221

Goetchius Wetland Preserve

48.

Goetchius Wetland Preserve

Location:	Caroline, Tompkins County
Directions:	From Ithaca, head southeast on Route 79. Turn north onto Flat Iron Road. In 0.2 mile park along the edge of the road, past a silver metal roofed building, and just before (south of) a creek. N42° 22.940 - W76° 18.037
Hiking Time:	30 minute loop
Length:	0.5-mile loop
Difficulty:	
Surface:	Woods trail (no definitive treadway to follow, but it's well blazed)
Trail Markings:	Blue and yellow blazes
Uses:	
Dogs:	OK on leash
Contact:	Finger Lakes Land Trust
	202 East Court Street, Ithaca, NY 14850
	(607) 275-9487 www.fllt.org

Here's a short, easy stroll through Mary's Woods, named after Mary Willsey, a previous owner of the woods. Mary's Woods is the forest portion of the Mabel P. and Paul T. Goetchius Wetland Preserve which is composed of 36 acres of wetland and hardwood forest.

Trail Directions
- From Flat Iron Road cross the grass just south of the shrubs (it's a right-of-way), and enter the woods at the "Mary's Woods" sign.
- Follow the blue blazes for a loop trail or extend it a bit by including the yellow trail.

Date Hiked: _____

Notes:

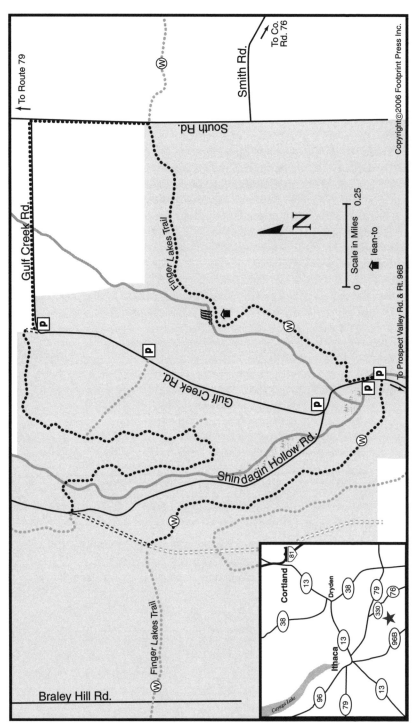

Shidagin Hollow State Forest

49.

Shindagin Hollow State Forest

Location: Caroline, Tompkins County

Directions: From Ithaca, head east on Route 79 for 7.4 miles. After the Caroline Elementary School, turn south onto Boiceville Road. At the end, turn left onto Valley Road / Central Chapel Road. Bear left at the "Y" onto Shindagin Hollow Road. Pass Gulf Greek Road, and park in the valley, near a wooden bridge where the Finger Lakes Trail crosses the road.
N42º 19.321 - W76º 19.951

Alternative Parking: A larger parking area is south a bit more on Shindagin Hollow Road, across the road from where the Finger Lakes Trail pops out of the woods from the west.
N42º 19.230 - W76º 19.931

Alternative Parking: You can also park near the bend in Gulf Creek Road (N42º 20.161- W76º 19.747) and farther south along Gulf Creek Road near a side trail. (N42º 19.859 - W76º 19.883.)

Hiking Time: 3 hour loop

Length: 5.3-mile loop
(Shindagin Hollow has a much more extensive network of trails that are used by mountain bikers. For a detailed map see *Take Your Bike - Family Rides in the Finger Lakes Region.*)

Difficulty: 👣 👣 👣 👣

Surface Woods trails, dirt roads, a small segment of paved road

Trail Markings: White blazes on the Finger Lakes Trail

Uses: 🚶

Dogs: OK

Contact: Finger Lakes Trail Conference
6111 Visitor Center Road, Mt. Morris, NY 14510
(585) 658-9320   www.fingerlakestrail.org

NYS Department of Environmental Conservation
1285 Fisher Avenue, Cortland, NY 13045
(607) 753-3095 ext. 215   www.dec.state.ny.us

Shindagin Hollow is a long, deep north-south valley, almost gorge-like in appearance. It was once the site of a well-used Native American trail that connected two other active trails — the Onondaga-Owego Trail and the Cayuga-Owego Trail.

Today it's a state forest, known as "The Promised Land" to mountain bikers. It's crossed by miles of challenging singletrack filled with roots, rocks, steep climbs and mind-blowing descents. The Finger Lakes Trail winds through this forest and offers a hikers-only option for enjoying this rugged terrain.

Trail Directions
- From the small pull-off in the valley on Shindagin Hollow Road, cross the wooden bridge, heading north on the white-blazed Finger Lakes Trail.
- Head uphill to a shelter in a pine forest at N42º 19.669 - W76º 19.734.
- Continue along the creek edge, and pass a waterfall.
- When you reach paved South Road, turn left and follow it.
- Turn left onto dirt Gulf Creek Road.
- When Gulf Creek Road bends south, look for a an old dirt road heading north.
- Follow this road as it turns into a trail and swings south.
- There's a steep downhill to cross the creek then a steep uphill to Shindagin Hollow Road.
- Cross Shindagin Hollow Road and follow the jeep trail southwest, under the shade of large trees.
- Watch for the white blazes where the Finger Lakes Trail crosses the jeep trail and turn left (E) onto the trail.
- Follow the edge of a cliff.
- There's a steep descent to Shindagin Hollow Road.
- Turn left, and follow Shindagin Hollow Road north to the pull-off near the bridge.

Date Hiked: _____

Notes:

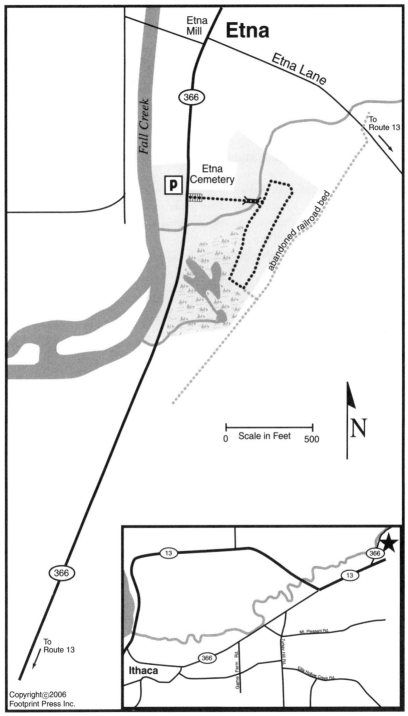

Etna Nature Preserve

50.

Etna Nature Preserve

Location:	Etna, Tompkins County
Directions:	From Ithaca, head northeast on Route 366. Continue east as it joins Route 13. Turn left (N) onto Route 366, and watch for an unmarked dirt loop parking area on the left in about a mile, across from Etna Cemetery. N42º 29.011 - W76º 23.043
Hiking Time:	30 minute loop
Length:	0.5-mile loop
Difficulty:	👣 👣
Surface:	Woods trail
Trail Markings:	None
Uses:	🚶 🎿
Dogs:	OK on leash
Contact:	Finger Lakes Land Trust 202 East Court Street, Ithaca, NY 14850 (607) 275-9487 www.fllt.org

Etna Nature Preserve is 11 acres of bird preserve donated by Walter and Sally Spofford in 1991. The short, easy loop trail crosses a bridge over a stream and wetland, then loops around a higher level coniferous forest. A connector trail leads to a portion of an abandoned railroad bed where wooden ties and iron rails can still be found. In addition to an abundance of birds, we found mayapples and other spring forest flowers and lots of rabbits when we hiked in spring.

Trail Directions
- From the parking area, head south along Route 366 to the edge of the cemetery. Cross the road and start the trail on a boardwalk at the green and white "no hunting" sign.
- Cross the stream on a bridge, then climb the opposite bank. You can loop either left or right.

Date Hiked: _____

Notes:

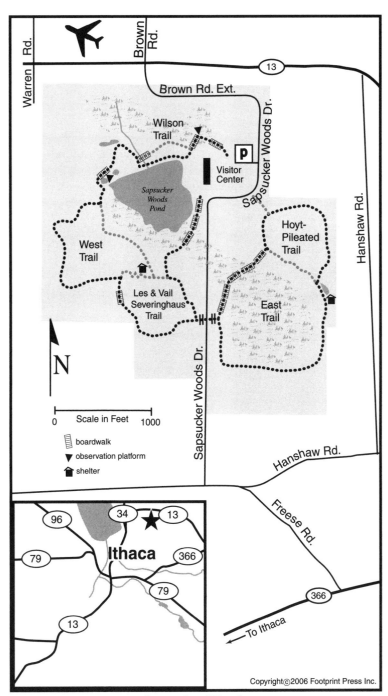

Sapsucker Woods

51.

Sapsucker Woods

Location:	East of Ithaca, Tompkins County
Directions:	From Route 13 north, heading east from the south end of Cayuga Lake, turn right (S) on Brown Road Extension. Turn right on Sapsucker Woods Drive. The parking area will be on the right. N42° 28.807 - W76° 27.050
Hiking Time:	1.25 hour loop
Length:	2.5-mile loop
Difficulty:	👟
Surface:	Mulched trails
Trail Markings:	None (some intersections have posted maps)
Uses:	🚶
Dogs:	Pets NOT allowed
Contact:	Sapsucker Woods
	Cornell Laboratory of Ornithology
	159 Sapsucker Woods Drive, Ithaca, NY 14851
	(80) 843-2473 www.birds.cornell.edu/

You won't want to hurry on this trail. The raised mulch foot bed makes for a soft walk as you wander through the woods past ponds. The area is alive with wildlife. Close to the visitor center, the trails have voice boxes. Press a button and you'll learn about the wildlife and vegetation of the area.

The Cornell Lab of Ornithology is open Monday through Thursday 8 AM to 5 PM, Friday 8 AM to 4 PM, and Saturday 10 AM to 4 PM. Trails are always open; simply close the gates behind you. Within the Cornell Lab of Ornithology is the Lyman K. Stuart Observatory, where you can sit and watch birds through a large window overlooking the ten-acre pond and listen to their calls piped in through microphones. During Cornell's spring and fall semesters, the Lab presents Monday evening seminars, featuring lectures by ornithologists, birders, authors, photographers, and other people who have worked extensively with birds. The Lab also houses

A welcoming entrance into Sapsucker Woods.

a superb collection of bird paintings by famed artist Louis Agassiz Fuertes and an excellent birding shop run by Wild Birds Unlimited.

Trail Directions

- From the parking area near the Visitor Center, pass through the gate on Wilson Trail heading north.
- Bear left, past a trail to the right.
- Reach the pond.
- Continue straight where the small loop trail joins from the right.
- Reach a boardwalk. Turn left for a short walk to an observation platform over the wetlands.
- Turn right at the next intersection onto the West Trail.
- Reach a "T" and turn right. (Right goes to a private area.)
- At 0.6 mile, cross a wooden bridge.
- Turn right on the Les & Vail Severinghaus Trail.
- Cross a boardwalk.
- At 1.0 mile, pass a trail to the left. (That trail would return you to the Visitor center for a shorter 1.3-mile hike.) Continue straight across Sapsucker Woods Drive and through the gate on the other side.
- Reach a "T" at 1.1 miles, and turn right (S) on the East Trail.
- Pass a pond.
- At a "Y," bear left. (The trail straight goes to a bench.)
- Reach a shelter and pond. Check for frogs and turtles on the logs.

•At 1.6 miles bear right at a "Y," onto the Hoyt-Pileated Trail, then cross a narrow boardwalk.
•Bear left at a "Y." (Right is a service entrance.)
•At 1.9 miles bear right over a boardwalk through a fern-filled swamp.
•At 2.1 miles, reach a "Y" and bear right. Cross Sapsucker Woods Drive and pass through the gates on the other side.
•Turn right at the first junction onto the Les & Vail Severinghaus Trail.
•Bear right at the "Y."
•Cross a boardwalk.
•Pass through a gate and continue straight to the parking area.

Date Hiked: _____

Notes:

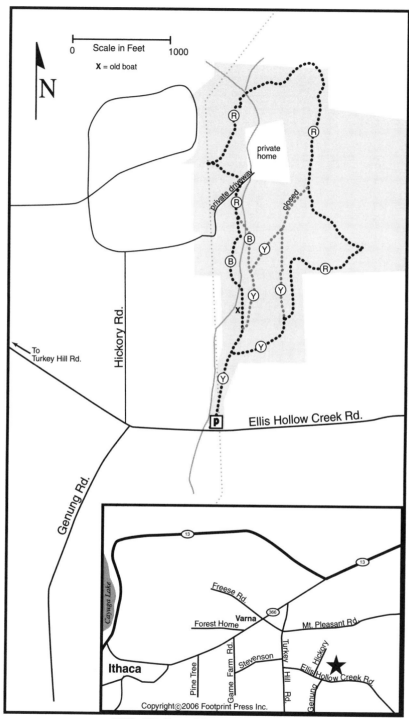

Ellis Hollow Nature Preserve

52.

Ellis Hollow Nature Preserve

Location:	Dryden, Tompkins County
Directions:	From Ithaca, head northeast on Route 366. Turn right (S) onto Mt. Pleasant Road then right (S) again onto Turkey Hill Road. Turn left (E) onto Ellis Hollow Creek Road. The parking area is on the left after Genung/Hickory Roads. N42° 26.306 - W76° 24.594
Hiking Time:	45 minute loop
Length:	1.5-mile perimeter loop
	Red Trail: 1.0 mile
	Blue Trail: 0.3 mile
	Yellow Trail: 0.5 mile
Difficulty:	👣 👣 👣
Surface:	Woods trail
Trail Markings:	Colored blazes
Uses:	🚶 🥾
Dogs:	OK on leash
Contact:	Finger Lakes Land Trust
	202 East Court Street, Ithaca, NY 14850
	(607) 275-9487 www.fllt.org

Long-time residents of the area, Barbara Keeton and her family, donated these 111 acres in 2000, so it's available for all of us to enjoy. Don't be fooled by the start of the trail. It passes through a NYSEG power line right-of-way, but soon you'll be in a magical forest of oaks, maples, hickories, basswoods, black cherries, white ashes and black birches. The preserve hugs the flanks of a hollow formed by Mt. Pleasant and Snyder Hill with a tributary of Cascadilla Creek flowing through its trough. That means you're bound to do some climbing on these trails. The mildest one is the blue trail which follows the creekbed. There are no bridges for creek crossings, so bring a walking stick for balance, particularly in spring.

Because of the uneven terrain, only the lower portion was ever cultivated. Deer are plentiful here, and it's not unusual to see red fox. Look for an old boat along the blue trail. It has sat on this spot for decades, and probably will for several more as nature takes its course.

Trail Directions

- From the parking area, head north on the right-of-way along the yellow trail. If you time it right, the fragrant honeysuckle will be in bloom and the wild strawberries will be ripe.
- At the first trail junction, near the kiosk, bear right, still following yellow.
- At the next junction turn right on the red trail.
- Pass the former gully trail (now closed for restoration) on the left, and continue climbing. The red trail will swing left then eventually head south.
- Pass a driveway to a private residence.
- At the blue trail junction you can go either direction. They both continue south along the tributary creek to meet the yellow trail.
- At the yellow trail turn right, and follow it back to the parking area.

Date Hiked: _____

Notes:

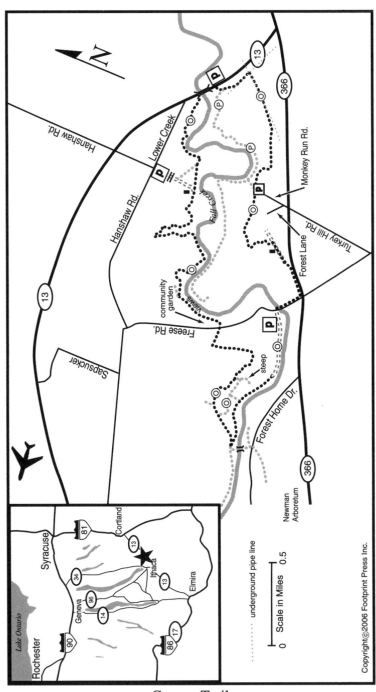

Cayuga Trail

53.

Cayuga Trail

Location: Ithaca, Tompkins County
Directions: From Route 366 (west of the junction with Route 13), turn north on Monkey Run Road. Park at the end of the road, on the left, before the barricade and in front of a sign, "No Parking – Snow Plow Turnaround." N42° 27.806- W76° 25.623 Do not park here if it's likely to snow while you're out.
Alternative Parking: Along the gravel road north of Fall Creek off Freese Road. N42° 27.427 - W76° 26.344
Alternative Parking: CRC (Cornell Recreation Community) Park at the intersection of Hanshaw Road and Lower Creek Road. Room for ~8 cars. N42° 28.315 - W76° 25.838
Alternative Parking: On the east side of Route 13, south of Fall Creek. N42° 28.299 - W76° 25.145
Hiking Time: 3 hour loop
Length: 6.5-mile loop
Difficulty: 👣 👣 👣 👣
Surface: Dirt trails
Trail Markings: Orange blazes
Uses: 🚶 🎿
Dogs: OK on leash
Contact: Cayuga Trails Club
P.O. Box 754, Ithaca, NY 14851-0754
www.lightlink.com/ctc/

Brothers Richard Hanks, age 11, and Kenneth Hanks, age 14, established portions of this trail in 1945. The area around Fall Creek was called Monkey Run and was popular for hunting, fishing, trapping, and swimming. The Scotch Pine grove you'll hike through was planted with defective European stock and never did particularly well. The abandoned rail bed you'll walk carried coal to the Cornell University heating plant in the 1940s.

The cliffs above Fall Creek.

The trail described has short road walk sections, but the rest is through dense woods with spectacular hills to climb, valley views, and walks along a wide, gurgling creek.

Trail Directions
•From the end of Monkey Run Road, head left (W) on the orange-blazed trail.
•Turn right (W) on a small gravel road and pass a block pump house on the right.
•Turn right (SW) onto Route 366 and follow it for 0.2 mile.
•Turn right (NW) onto Freese Road and follow it for 0.1 mile over the bridge.
•Turn left (W) onto a gravel farm road toward the sign "No Parking – Snow Plow Turnaround."
•The gravel road turns to a dirt lane along the edge of a field. Blazes are sporadic in this section.
•Continue straight and enter the woods. (You will not see the trail to the right. It is hidden behind brush.) The creek will be to your left.
•Pass a trail to the right.
•Turn right (E) and head away from the creek. (Left heads to the suspension bridge over Fall Creek to Newman Arboretum.)
•Climb a steep hill.

Looking down to Fall Creek.

•Pass an orange trail to the right (almost all trails in this area are orange-blazed).
•Pass an unmarked trail to the left. Continue straight following orange blazes.
•Pass another trail to the right. (Right heads down a steep hill to the field at the end of the gravel road taken earlier from the Freese Road bridge.)
•Enter a field. Turn right and follow orange blazes along the edge of the field and woods.
•At 3.2 miles, turn right onto a gravel double-track.
•Continue straight on a paved path, and at 3.3 miles cross Freese Road.
•Walk along the back of a field containing a community garden. The cliff and creek are below on your right.
•Watch for the trail to turn right into the woods at N42º 27.746 - W76º 26.605.
•The trail turns right, staying next to the gorge with gorgeous views. (A side trail goes straight.)
•Exit the woods and turn right (E) along a field.
•Re-enter the woods at N42º 28.138 - W76º 26.194 and descend.
•At 3.9 miles, reach the bottom of the gorge and turn left (E).

- Climb out of the gorge.
- At 4.3 miles, exit the woods.
- Turn right, cross grass, and re-enter the woods in 100 yards.
- Pass a lookout over the creek.
- Reach a "Y" at 4.4 miles. Bear left, then cross an intersection.
- Cross a wide cinder trail. Quickly reach a "T" at the edge of a cliff and turn left. The creek will be on your right, far below.
- Walk steeply downhill, cross a seasonal streambed, then head uphill.
- Head downhill, then cross a seasonal streambed.
- Reach the creek and bear left.
- Pass a trail to a house on the left.
- At 4.7 miles, reach Route 13. Turn right and cross on the bridge.
- Immediately after the bridge, turn right and head downhill across a field on a mowed strip, then into woods.
- Pass a pink side trail. (This dead-end trail leads to great views of the spires along Fall Creek.)
- At 4.8 miles, reach an abandoned railroad bed and turn right onto the wide mowed path.
- Pass a house on the left. Blazes are sporadic.
- At 4.9 miles, the orange-blazed trail turns right into the woods. The cliff to the creek will be on your right.
- Pass a trail to the right. Continue following orange blazes as the trail bends left.
- Cross a streambed.
- Cross a small wooden bridge and reach a "T."
- Turn left, pass the barricade, and reach the parking area.

Date Hiked: _____

Notes:

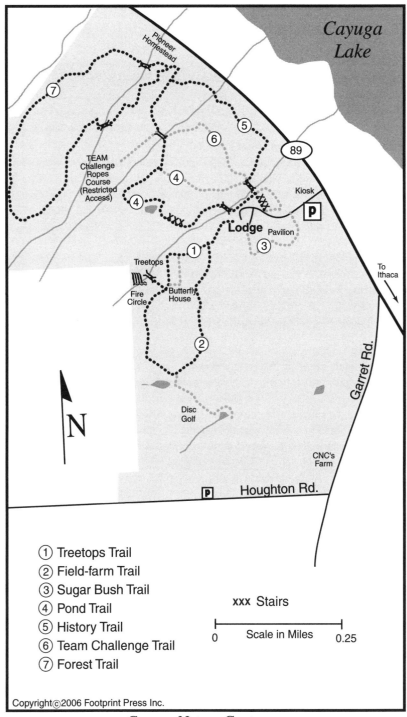

① Treetops Trail
② Field-farm Trail
③ Sugar Bush Trail
④ Pond Trail
⑤ History Trail
⑥ Team Challenge Trail
⑦ Forest Trail

xxx Stairs

Scale in Miles
0 ———————— 0.25

Copyright© 2006 Footprint Press Inc.

Cayuga Nature Center

54.

Cayuga Nature Center

Location:	Ithaca, Tompkins County
Directions:	From Ithaca, head north on Route 89 for 6 miles. Cayuga Nature Center will be on the left (W). N43º 31.130 - W76º 33.308

Alternative Parking: Off Houghton Road N43º 30.776 - W76º 33.502

Length:	Total: 5 miles of trails
Surface:	Woods trails
Trail Markings:	Colored plastic markers
Dogs:	Pets are NOT allowed
Admission:	$3 adults, $2 students & seniors, $1 kids aged 2 to 11
Contact:	Cayuga Nature Center
	1420 Taughannock Blvd., Ithaca, NY 14850
	(607) 273-6260 www.cayuganaturecenter.org

Explore the wonders of the natural world first hand. The Cayuga Nature Center houses over 30 live animals in both indoor and outdoor exhibits. Explore the Butterfly House seasonally from June to August. Climb 50 feet into the tree canopy at Treetops, a six story observational treehouse. Or simply enjoy the outdoors while walking the five miles of interpretive trails, which meander through a mature deciduous forest, along gorges and streams, and past a variety of native plants and wildlife on the nature center's 135 acres of land. Public nature programs are offered every Sunday afternoon.

Cayuga Nature Center grounds are open dawn to dusk, 365 days a year. The main lodge is open summers from June through August, 9 AM to 5 PM. During fall, winter, and spring, the hours are 10 AM to 3 PM. Please do not feed any of the animals, and be aware that the farm fences are electrified.

Trail	Distance	Level of Difficulty
1. Treetops Trail	0.2 mile	2 boots, wheelchair accessible

    Pass Gaji the hawk on your way to the observation tower. Side trails lead to the butterfly house, the fire circle and a waterfall overlook.

Trail	Distance	Level of Difficulty

2. Field Trail 0.4 mile 2 boots, wheelchair accessible
Pass bluebird boxes, wetlands, ponds, and wildflowers. From June to
August the trail features an enclosed butterfly house which is accessible by wheelchair and stroller.

3. Sugarbush Trail 0.2 mile 2 boots
Leads to the sugar shack where maple syrup is produced in early spring.

4. Pond Trail 0.7 mile loop 3 boots
Explore the gorge and pass a vernal pond.

5. History Trail 0.3 mile 2 boots
Hike along the stream to the pioneer homestead.

6. Team Challenge Trail 0.4 mile
Leads to the restricted team challenge ropes course.

7. Forest Trail 1.1 miles 3 boots
Hike through a shaded mature hardwood forest.

8. Compost Trail 0.2 mile 2 boots
Leads to the CNC composting center.

Recommended loop hike on Trails 1 & 2

Hiking Time: 30 minute loop
Length: 0.75-mile loop
Difficulty: 👢👢

Uses: 🚶 🎿 ♿

Date Hiked: _____

Notes:

Recommended loop hike on Trails 5, 7 and 4

Hiking Time:	1 hour loop
Length:	2-mile loop
Difficulty:	👣 👣 👣
Uses:	🚶 ⛷

Date Hiked: _____

Notes:

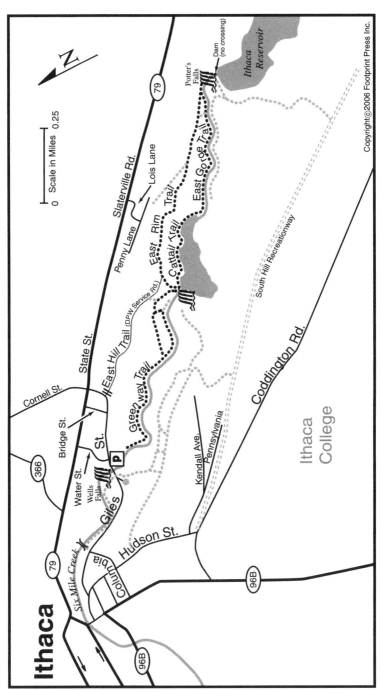

Six-Mile Creek Trail

55.

Six-Mile Creek Trail

Location:	Ithaca, Tompkins County
Directions:	In Ithaca, take Route 79 east, past Route 366. Turn right onto Giles Street. Just before the bridge over Six-Mile Creek, turn left into a parking area. It's marked by a brown sign "Mulholland Wildflower Preserve" and a white sign "VanNattas Dam Watershed Area." N42º 25.955 - W76º 29.057
Hiking Time:	2.5 hours round trip
Length:	4.8 miles round trip
Difficulty:	🥾🥾🥾🥾
Surface:	Dirt trail
Trail Markings:	Sign at entrance only
Uses:	🚶 🎿
Dogs:	OK on leash, clean up after pet
Contact:	City of Ithaca, DPW, Parks & Forestry 245 Pier Road, Ithaca, NY 14850 www.ci.ithaca.ny.us

Six-Mile Creek, particularly above the dam and at Potter's Falls (also called Green Tree Falls), is a notorious nude sunbathing and skinny dipping area. But beware, swimming is not allowed here. The area is patrolled by the Gorge Rangers who can arrest swimmers. Too bad, the allure is almost too much to resist.

Even so, the walk to this waterfall is a very pleasant hike through woods. In spring you'll see waterfalls in tributaries as well as Six-Mile Creek. Along the creek bed and deep in the woods you'll find many old water pipes dating from the early 1900s. This creek is still used as Ithaca's water source—hence the no-swimming rule.

Across Giles Street is the VanNattas Dam, which sits above a natural waterfall called Wells Falls or Business Man's Lunch Falls. This waterfall and many others are described in *200 Waterfalls in Central and Western New York - A Finders' Guide.*

Trail Directions:
- From the parking area head south across a wooden bridge toward the creek.
- Walk upstream on a mulched trail (Greenway Trail) parallel to the creek.
- At 0.5 mile, pass a side trail to the left. Continue straight.
- At 0.6 mile, look across the creek at a wide dirt area. In spring a waterfall tumbles down to Six-Mile Creek. Also look upstream on Six-Mile Creek to see your first small waterfall.
- The side loop trail comes in on the left, but continue straight.
- The trail will narrow. Continue straight until you can see a small dam with an 8-foot cascade. Just beyond it is a larger dam with a 30-foot freefall waterfall. (The two dams help minimize siltation problems in the drinking water.) This is as far as you can go on this trail.
- Backtrack to the last side trail and turn right, away from the creek.
- Shortly, in the woods, turn right and take the trail uphill, heading north.
- Reach a junction at 1.1 miles, and turn right (E).
- At 1.2 miles cross a tributary creek (with waterfalls in spring).
- Pass the two dam falls far below.
- At the reservoir, turn left and head uphill. (The trail straight ahead will be part of your return loop.)
- At 1.5 miles turn right (E) onto an old gravel roadway (East Rim Trail).
- The roadway disappears and the trail narrows above a swampy reservoir pond.
- At 1.7 miles, cross a gully (with waterfalls in spring) on an old waterpipe.
- Climb a steep hill to get a great view from the end of the swampy reservoir pond.
- At the top of the hill, continue straight, downhill. (A trail to the left leads to houses.)
- At 2 miles, cross a gully that sports a 12-foot waterfall even in mid-June.
- Continue straight as a trail merges from houses.
- With the creek in view, turn left onto a side trail to stay upland on a trail that leads to Potter's Falls.
- The trail ends at Potter's Falls at 2.4 miles.

To Return:
- Put your back to the waterfall and turn left to take the trail down at water level (East Gorge Trail).
- Continue straight, passing several small side trails.
- At 2.8 miles pass a gully with a waterfall.
- Continue straight at water level (Cattail Trail), passing the swampy reservoir pond.
- At 3.4 miles climb a hill to get around the dam.

223

- Cross a gully at 3.7 miles (with waterfalls in spring).
- At 3.8 miles, turn left at a junction and head downhill.
- At the base of the hill, bear right, then turn right onto a wide dirt trail.
- Turn right when you reach the water's edge, and follow this trail (Greenway Trail) back to the parking area.

Date Hiked: _____

Notes:

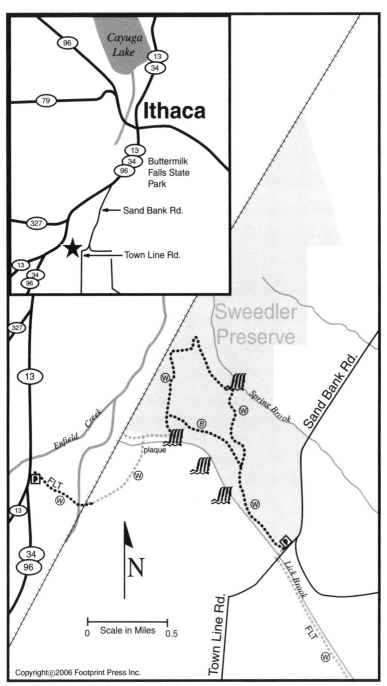

Sweedler Preserve

56.

Sweedler Preserve

Location:	South of Ithaca, Tompkins County
Directions:	From Ithaca, head south on Route 13/34/96. Just south of Buttermilk Falls State Park, turn left (S) on Sand Bank Road. Bear right onto Town Line Road. Park on the right side of the road near the Finger Lakes Trail sign. N42° 23.747 - W76° 31.984
Alternative Parking:	Parking area adjacent to confluence of Routes 13 and 34/96 N42° 23.897 - W76° 32.741
Hiking Time:	1 hour loop
Length:	1.4-mile loop
Difficulty:	👣 👣 👣 👣
Surface:	Dirt trail
Trail Markings:	White and blue blazes
Uses:	🚶
Dogs:	OK on leash
Contact:	Finger Lakes Land Trust 202 East Court Street, Ithaca, NY 14850 (607) 275-9487 www.fllt.org
	Cayuga Trails Club PO Box 754, Ithaca, NY 14851 www.lightlink.com/ctc
	Finger Lakes Trail Conference 6111 Visitor Center Road, Mt. Morris, NY 14510 (585) 658-9320 www.fingerlakestrail.org

Like much of the land in the Finger Lakes region, most of the Sweedler Preserve was cleared for farming after the Revolutionary War. However, poor soil led to abandonment of the farms and their return to forest. Since the 1800s, Lick Brook, which runs through the preserve, has been a popular picnic and hiking spot, primarily because of the many waterfalls. The Finger Lakes Land Trust acquired this unique land through a bargain sale from owners Moss and Kristin Sweedler in 1993. By selling the Lick Brook

One of the many Lick Brook waterfalls.

land for far below market value, the Sweedlers helped preserve this beautiful land and did us all an immense favor.

In its plummet to Cayuga Inlet, Lick Brook carved a deep gorge with dangerous cliffs. Please stay on the trail, away from cliff edges. In 2001, the Finger Lakes Trail, which runs through the preserve, was rerouted to provide a gentler climb up the hillside. White blazes denote the current Finger Lakes Trail. The steep trail along the edge of Lick Brook is now a blue-blazed side trail. To best view the waterfalls the trail directions instruct you to hike to the bottom of the valley following the white-blazed Finger Lakes Trail, then watch for waterfalls on your way back uphill along the blue-blazed trail. This will facilitate seeing the waterfalls without leaving the trail.

Trail Directions:
- From the parking area along Town Line Road, head downhill (NW), following the white blazes.
- Watch for the white-blazed trail to turn right. Continue following the white blazes to Spring Brook.
- At Spring Brook, turn left and follow the trail downhill, still marked by white blazes.

- When you reach the valley floor, follow the white blazes as they turn left toward Lick Brook.
- Leave the main trail to walk into the Lick Brook stream bed (if the water is low enough) to get a view of the bottom waterfall.
- Now, return to the trail and follow the blue-blazed trail steeply up the hill, watching to the right for the procession of waterfalls.
- Continue straight as the blazes turn to white and you pass the white trail to the left.
- You'll reach the parking area gasping for breath but sated with the beauty of Lick Brook.

Date Hiked: _____

Notes:

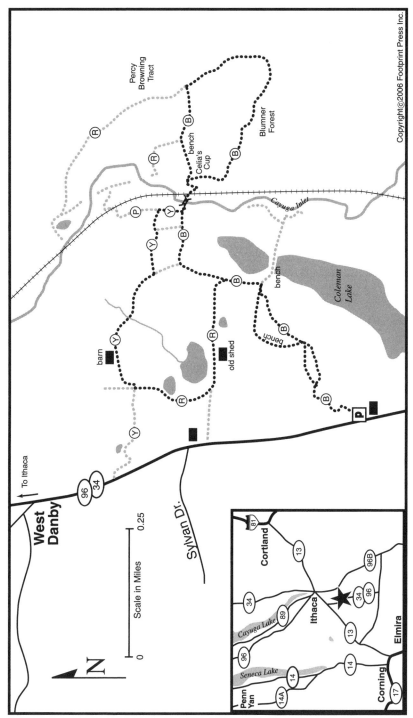

Lindsay-Parsons Biodiversity Preserve

57.

Lindsay-Parsons Biodiversity Preserve

Location:	West Danby, south of Ithaca, Tompkins County
Directions:	From Ithaca, head south on Route 13. Take the left exit onto Route 34/96. Continue about 7 miles. The parking area is 0.5-mile south of Sylvan Drive. It's on the left (E) side, opposite house #2500. N42° 18.549 - W76° 31.984
Hiking Time:	1.5 hour loop
Length:	3.1-mile loop (darkened trails on map)
	4.5 miles total trails
	Blue Trail: 1.7 miles
	Yellow Trail: 0.7 mile
	Pink Trail: 0.3 mile
	Eastern Red Trail: 0.8 mile (there are no bridges over Cayuga Inlet)
	Western Red Trail: 0.5 miles
Difficulty:	👟 👟 👟
Surface:	Mowed-grass and dirt trails
Trail Markings:	Colored blazes
Uses:	🚶 🎿
Dogs:	OK on leash
Contact:	Finger Lakes Land Trust
	202 East Court Street, Ithaca, NY 14850
	(607) 275-9487 www.fllt.org

For centuries, scientists have traveled the globe to exotic locales in search of plants and animals with medicinal qualities. In 1994 Professor Thomas Eisner of the Cornell Institute for Research in Chemical Ecology approached the Finger Lakes Land Trust with a request to find an ecologically diverse tract that could be used for a local search for useful chemicals in nature.

Land Trust forester Michael DeMunn found this parcel for sale and with donations from Elizabeth Kirchner (daughter of the Lindsay-Parsons) and others, the Lindsay-Parsons Preserve was born. Another major donor was

A bench overlooking Coleman Lake.

Edmond G. Blumner, in memory of his wife Celia. Additional land purchases and gifts have resulted in a preserve of nearly 500 acres.

Some of the natural diversity you'll find here includes:
-Rare endemic grass (Calamagrostis porteri, ssp. perplexa)
-Ospreys and great egrets on Coleman Lake
-Wild ginger and marsh marigold in the wetlands along Cayuga Inlet.
-Celia's Cup — a glacial kettle depression formed by a giant chunk of glacial ice.
-A mature forest of maple, basswood, and hemlock.
-Plenty of deer. Evidence has also been found of black bears and coyote on this land.

The Finger Lakes Land Trust formed a 3-year contract with Cornell and the Schering-Plough Pharmaceutical Corporation to use the Biodiversity preserve for bioprospectiong. We found it to be a wonderful spot for our own prospecting — to enjoy the sights, sounds, and smells of the natural world.

Trail Directions:
• From the parking area, follow the mowed-grass blue trail.
• Bear right to stay on the blue trail as a few side loops veer off to the left. (You can take them on your return trip.)

A creek flows through Lindsay-Parsons Biodiversity Preserve.

- Pass an unmarked, dead-end trail to the right, then the red trail to the left.
- Pass three more trails to the left.
- Cross Cayuga Inlet on a bridge, then cross the railroad tracks. (Watch for trains.)
- When the blue trail splits, bear right and follow it through Blumner Forest.
- Stay left on the blue trail when the red trail intersects.
- Cross back over the railroad tracks and Cayuga Outlet on the blue trail.
- Take the next right onto the yellow-blazed trail. Beware of poison ivy along this trail.
- Stay on yellow when the pink trail branches off to the right.
- Pass two unmarked trails to the left.
- Turn left onto the red trail. Mowed-grass paths will wind between ponds to meet the blue trail.
- Turn right onto the blue trail.
- From here to the parking area, taking the right trail option will lead you along side loops.

Date Hiked: _____

Notes:

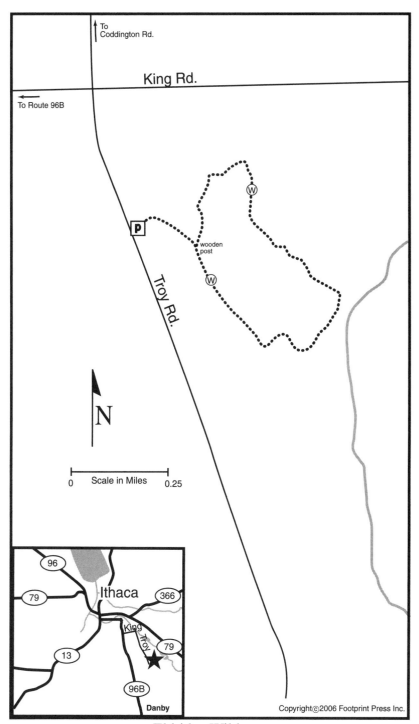

To
Coddington Rd.

King Rd.

To Route 96B

P

Troy Rd.

W

W

wooden
post

N

Scale in Miles
0   0.25

96

79

Ithaca

366

13

King

Troy

79

96B

Danby

Copyright©2006 Footprint Press Inc.

Eldridge Wilderness

58.

Eldridge Wilderness

Location:	South of Ithaca, Tompkins County
Directions:	From Ithaca, head south on Route 96B. Take a left (E) onto King Road and a right (S) onto Troy Road. A 2-car pull-off will be on the left near a white sign for Eldridge Wilderness. N42º 23.970 - W76º 28.570
Hiking Time:	45 minute loop
Length:	1.3-mile loop (darkened trails on map)
Difficulty:	👣 👣 👣
Surface:	Woods trail
Trail Markings:	White blazes
Uses:	🚶 🎿
Dogs:	Dogs are NOT permitted
Contact:	The Nature Conservancy
	1048 University Avenue, Rochester, NY 14607
	(585) 546-8030 http://nature.org/centralwestern

You're likely to have this 87-acre woods to yourself as you hike. It's not a heavily used area. Trails are rudimentary to minimize species disturbance. Follow the blazes carefully. You'll wander past lily of the valley patches, through a young deciduous forest to a pine forest, and past some deep ravines. Deer are abundant in these woods, and a few of the trees are labeled.

Trail Directions:
• From the parking area, follow the white blazes into the woods.
• At the wooden post you can go either left or right to complete the loop.

   Date Hiked: _____

   Notes:

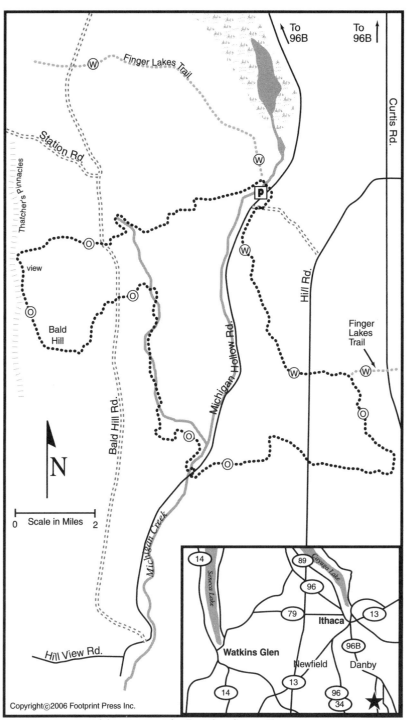

Abbott Loop in Danby State Forest

59.

Abbott Loop in Danby State Forest

Location:	Danby, Tompkins County
Directions:	From Ithaca, head south on Route 96B. In Danby turn right (S) onto Michigan Hollow Road, and watch to the right for the Finger Lakes Trail parking area. N42º 19.034 - W76º 28.661
Hiking Time:	4.5 hour loop
Length:	8.4-mile loop (darkened trail on map) (the orange-blazed segment is 6.7 miles)
Difficulty:	🥾🥾🥾🥾
Surface:	Dirt trail
Trail Markings:	Orange and white blazes
Uses:	🚶
Dogs:	OK on leash
Contact:	Finger Lakes Trail Conference 6111 Visitor Center Road, Mt. Morris, NY 14510 (585) 658-9320 www.fingerlakestrail.org

The Abbott Loop offers a well-marked, easy-to-follow, rugged day hike as a side loop to the Finger Lakes Trail. From Michigan Hollow Road you climb out of Michigan Creek Valley to gain a 180º panoramic view of the next valley from atop Bald Hill at Thather's Pinnacles. Then head back down to walk the ravine through Michigan Creek Valley, cross the valley and climb the opposite side, only to hike back down to complete the loop in Michigan Creek Valley. The maximum elevation change is 540 feet, but some sections are steep. It is a beautiful walk.

Trail Directions:
- From the parking area, follow the white blazes north to cross Michigan Creek on a bridge marked Diane's Crossing.
- Turn left and follow the orange-blazed trail. (The white-blazed Finger Lakes Trail heads straight.)
- Head uphill. Pass a bulldozed gravel area and several old logging roads.
- Descend into a valley, cross a stream, and climb again.
- Cross seasonal Bald Hill Road.

- The trail will bend south and offer view off Thatcher's Pinnacles.
- Head downhill through an aromatic hemlock forest.
- Cross Bald Hill Road again and descend steeply into a small creek valley.
- Proceed through the deep valley, crossing back and forth over the small creek.
- Head into woods with the creek below to the right.
- Cross the creek on a bridge at N42° 18.073 - W76° 29.320.
- Head uphill away from the creek in a young forest then descend into the creek's floodplain.
- Meet Michigan Hollow Road at N42° 17.779 - W76° 29.150. Turn right to follow the road. Watch for the trail to begin again across the road and climb.
- Cross Hill Road and descend into a shallow valley of a tributary of Miller Creek.
- Follow the stream to the junction with the white-blazed Finger Lakes Trail. Turn left onto the Finger Lakes Trail.
- Head uphill, cross Hill Road a second time.
- Reach a seasonal dirt road and turn right to follow it uphill. Watch left for the trail to head back into the woods.
- Cross Michigan Hollow Road to return to the parking area.

Date Hiked: _____

Notes:

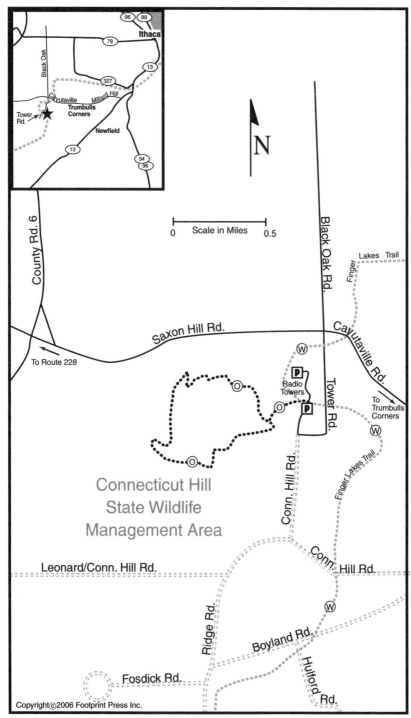

Bob Cameron Loop Trail

60.

Bob Cameron Loop Trail

Location:	Connecticut Hill State Wildlife Management Area, Tompkins County
Directions:	From Ithaca, head south on Route 13. One mile south of the Route 34/96 junction, turn west onto Millard Hill Road. Pass through Trumbulls Corners and continue straight onto Cayutaville Road. Turn left (S) onto Tower Road. Follow paved Tower Road around two sharp bends to the right, then park along the side of the road where the Finger Lakes Trail crosses. It's marked by a yellow and green Finger Lakes Trail sign. N42º 23.156 - W76º 40.123
Alternative Parking:	Park in the loop at the end of Tower Road and walk the road back to the trail crossing.
Hiking Time:	1.5 hour loop
Length:	2.7-mile loop
Difficulty:	🐾 🐾 🐾
Surface:	Dirt trail
Trail Markings:	Orange blazes
Uses:	🚶 🎿
Dogs:	OK on leash
Contact:	Finger Lakes Trail Conference
	6111 Visitor Center Road, Mt. Morris, NY 14510
	(585) 658-9320 www.fingerlakestrail.org
	Cayuga Trails Club
	PO Box 754, Ithaca, NY 14851
	www.lightlink.com/ctc

The Cayuga Trails Club developed the Bob Cameron Loop Trail as an off-shoot of the Finger Lakes Trail to honor Bob Cameron, a long-time caretaker of the Connecticut Hill State Wildlife Management Area. It's a pleasant woods walk through a forest floor covered in ferns and mayapples in spring. Take along a fern identification book and see how many varieties you can find. Part of the walk parallels a small ravine then wanders through a pine forest.

We recommend entering Connecticut Hill State Wildlife Management Area from the north. The roads from the south are extremely rough.

Trail Directions:
• From where the white-blazed Finger Lakes Trail crosses Tower Road, head west into the woods.
• Shortly, turn left and follow the orange-blazed trail. (The white blazed Finger Lakes Trail heads straight.)
• Follow the orange blazes until they loop you back to the white-blazed Finger Lakes Trail.
• Turn right and follow the Finger Lakes Trail back to Tower Road.

    Date Hiked: _____

    Notes:

Walks in Schuyler & Steuben Counties

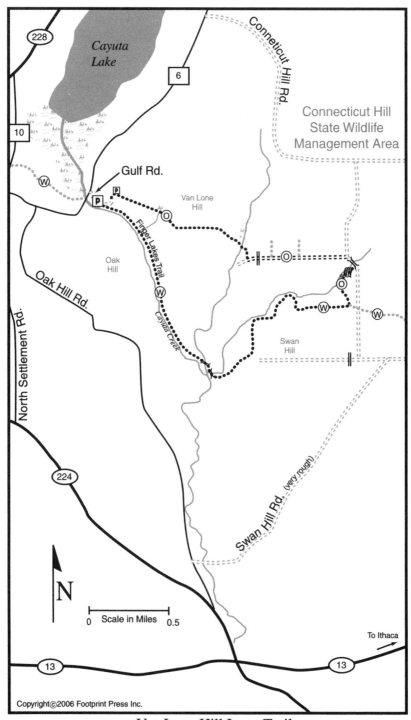

Van Lone Hill Loop Trail

61.

Van Lone Hill Loop Trail

Location: South of Cayuta Lake, Schuyler County
Directions: From Route 228, southwest of Cayuta Lake, turn
south onto County Road 10 (N. Settlement Road),
then left (E) onto County Road 6. County Road 6 will
turn a sharp left bend and cross Cayuta Creek. Shortly
after the creek, turn right onto dirt Gulf Road. Park
along the road where the Finger Lakes Trail heads into
the woods on the right.
N42° 20.969 - W76° 44.229
Alternative Parking: Continue to the end of Gulf Road, up the steep dirt
road. There's room for 1 car in front of the large rocks
that make the road a dead end.
N42° 20.974 - W76° 43.897
Hiking Time: 3 hour loop
Length: 6.1-mile loop
Difficulty: 👣 👣 👣 👣

Surface: Dirt trail
Trail Markings: Orange and white blazes
Uses:

🚶

Dogs: OK on leash
Contact: Finger Lakes Trail Conference
6111 Visitor Center Road, Mt. Morris, NY 14510
(585) 658-9320 www.fingerlakestrail.org

Cayuga Trails Club
PO Box 754, Ithaca, NY 14851
www.lightlink.com/ctc

Take an aerobic hike through gorgeous woods, up some significant hills,
and walk beside creeks with cascading waterfalls. Watch for small orange
efts along the trail.

Ignore side trails along the way. Stick to the well-blazed orange and white
trails, and you'll have no problem following the Van Lone Hill Loop Trail.

The serene woods of Van Lone Hill.

Trail Directions:
- From either parking spot on Gulf Road, follow the road uphill to its end.
- Continue past the rocks on the orange-blazed trail, climbing Van Lone Hill.
- Head down into a creek valley where you'll probably have to hop on rocks to cross the small creek.
- When the trail meets a dirt road, turn left and follow the dirt road, passing some yellow gates.
- Bear right at a road junction, and cross a bridge over a creek.
- After the bridge, the orange trail veers right, into the woods, to a deep gully next to small cascading waterfalls.
- Meet the white-blazed Finger Lakes Trail, and turn right.
- Climb to a pine forest.
- Pass old stone foundations along the trail on the right, then on the left. N42° 20.035 - W76° 42.983
- Cross a log bridge, then another bridge. This is a great place for a refreshing break. Maybe even sit in the cascading water to cool off?
- Follow the white-blazed Finger Lakes Trail along Cayuta Creek all the way to Gulf Road.

    Date Hiked: _____

    Notes:

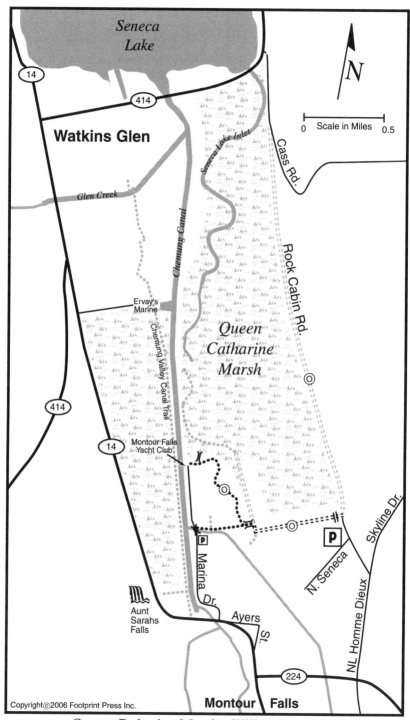

Queen Catharine Marsh - Willow Walk Trail

62.

~~~

Queen Catharine Marsh – Willow Walk Trail

Location:	Montour Falls at the south end of Seneca Lake, Schuyler County
Directions:	Take Route 14 south through Watkins Glen. At the north end of Montour Falls, turn east on Route 224. Turn left onto NL Homme Dieux, then left again onto Rock Cabin Road. Take a third left onto North Seneca Street. On the right, near this corner, is a grass parking area lined in stones. N42° 21.456 - W76° 50.393

Alternative Parking: Off Marina Drive, near the first bridge.
N42° 21.367 - W76° 51.173

Hiking Time:	1 hour loop
Length:	2.1-mile loop
Difficulty:	👞
Surface:	Dirt trails
Trail Markings:	Most of route is orange-blazed
Uses:	🚶
Dogs:	OK
Contact:	N.Y.S. Department of Environmental Conservation 7291 Coon Road, Bath, NY 14810-9728 (607) 776-2165 ext. 10 www.dec.state.ny.us

Queen Catharine Marsh is an 882-acre protected wetland. Its man-made ditches and potholes attract shorebirds, waterfowl, muskrats, and turtles, among other wildlife. The wetlands act as a natural sponge for floodwaters, absorbing thousands of gallons of floodwater per acre. Thirty species of butterflies breed in this area.

Once called Bad Indian Swamp, this cattail swamp at the south end of Seneca Lake was saved from the ravages of developers and swamp-pavers. Its current name is a tribute to a local native tribal monarch, Queen Catharine Montour, who died in 1804.

The Chemung Canal, which bisects Queen Catharine Marsh, once reached 23 miles south to Elmira. It was closed in 1887. The portion remaining today is part of the N. Y. S. Erie Canal System.

Willow Walk follows tree-shaded dikes through the wetland and passes large willow trees as it wanders through a lush green woods. This is an ideal short stroll for a hot summer day, but be sure to bring mosquito repellent.

Trail Directions
- From the parking area on N. Seneca, walk back up the road, and take a left onto Rock Cabin Road.
- Shortly, turn left onto a double track dirt and grass road, and pass a metal gate.
- You're heading west along the south end of Queen Catharine Marsh.
- Shortly after the road bends right, leave the road and turn left to cross a bridge, and bear right onto an orange-blazed trail.
- Pass a bridge to the right, but continue straight until you reach the cul-de-sac at the end of Marina Drive.
- Turn left and follow Marina Drive south.
- Just before the bridge, turn left and climb up the dike of a retention pond.
- Continue straight until you meet the double-track service road.
- Turn right, and follow the service road back to the parking area.

Date Hiked: _____

Notes:

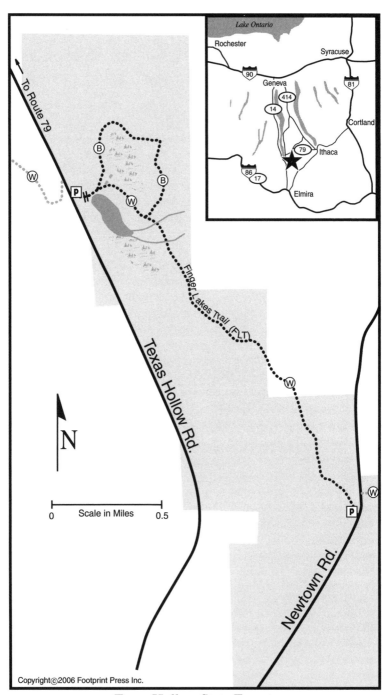

Texas Hollow State Forest

63.

Texas Hollow State Forest

Location:	Southeast of Seneca Lake, Schuyler County
Directions:	From Watkins Glen, follow Route 79 north. Pass through Burdett, then turn south on Texas Hollow Road. Park in front of the yellow metal barrier with a stop sign on the east side of Texas Hollow Road. It's a 1-to-2 car pull-off. N42º 24.756 - W76º 47.528
Alternative Parking:	A 1-to-2 car pull-off at the trail intersection on Newtown Road. N42º 24.771 - W76º 47.525
Hiking Time:	2.25 hour loop
Length:	4.1-mile loop
Difficulty:	👣 👣 👣 👣
Surface:	Dirt trails
Trail Markings:	Blue and white blazes
Uses:	🚶
Dogs:	OK on leash
Contact:	Finger Lakes Trail Conference
	6111 Visitor Center Road, Mt. Morris, NY 14510
	(585) 658-9320 www.fingerlakestrail.org
	N.Y.S. Department of Environmental Conservation
	7291 Coon Road, Bath, NY 14810-9728
	(607) 776-2165 ext. 10 www.dec.state.ny.us

This trail begins deceptively easily with a stroll around a pond and wetland, through a varied forest. It's fairly level for awhile, then the long and moderately steep climb to Newtown Road is sure to get your heart pounding. This trail is a fine example of wilderness tranquility and pure joy to hike.

Most of the route follows the Finger Lakes Trail. Its white blazes are easy to follow. As a side loop, you'll follow blue blazes around a wetland area. The blue blazes are more of a challenge to follow, and the path is less traveled. Be sure to pay attention to the blazes, and look behind you or backtrack to the last blaze if you find you've lost them. At one point you'll reach a logging road with no blazes in sight. Turn right, and they'll pick up again.

The goal is to keep the wetland to your right. It's not difficult to follow, it just requires attentiveness.

Trail Directions

- From the yellow barrier, follow the white blazes downhill (SE) on the wide path.
- Pass the edge of a pond on the right. The hill in front of you is the one you will climb.
- Bear right (E) at the "Y" following the white blazes.
- At 0.2 mile, reach the blue-blazed trail and turn left.
- Follow the blazes carefully through the woods, keeping the wetland to your right.
- Reach an old logging road and turn right. The blue blazes will begin again.
- At 0.9 mile, reach a "T" with the white-blazed trail. Turn left.
- Cross two rustic log bridges.
- The trail meanders through a pine forest and begins climbing steadily uphill.
- Cross several old logging roads and continue uphill after each.
- At 2.0 miles, the trail bends south to follow an old logging road for a short distance, then heads left (SE), uphill off the road.
- Reach Newtown Road at 2.3 miles. Turn around and head back downhill, following the white blazes.
- At 3.7 miles, pass the blue-blazed trail on the right.
- Pass the blue-blazed trail again at 3.9 miles.
- Pass the edge of the pond, then head uphill to the parking area at the yellow barrier.

Date Hiked: _____

Notes:

To Lodi

Dean Rd.   Covert Rd.   Fox Rd.

County Rd. 137

Keady Rd.

Townsendville Rd.

Parmenter Rd.   Butcher Hill Rd.   Clark Rd.

E. Townline Rd.

Lodi Center Rd.

P

Ames Rd.

Ⓞ

Trail   Ⓨ
            Trail

Cty. Rd. 146

Wilkens Rd.   Townsend Rd.

Cty. Rd. 143

Ⓞ

Interloken   No-Tan-Takto

Ⓨ

Case Rd.

Seneca Rd.   Seneca Rd.

P

Corners Rd.

No-Tan-Takto Trail   Ⓨ

Ⓞ *Teeter Pond*

Vesa Rd.

Cty. Rd. 1   (Searsburg Rd.)

Wardner

P   Ballard Pond Fishing Area

Interloken Trail

Potomac Rd.

Voorheis Rd.

Ⓨ

Ball Diamond   Backbone   Trail   P Chicken

Coop Rd.

Backbone

Ⓞ

0   Scale in Miles   1

N

Copyright© 2006 Footprint Press Inc.

Finger Lakes National Forest (North Section)

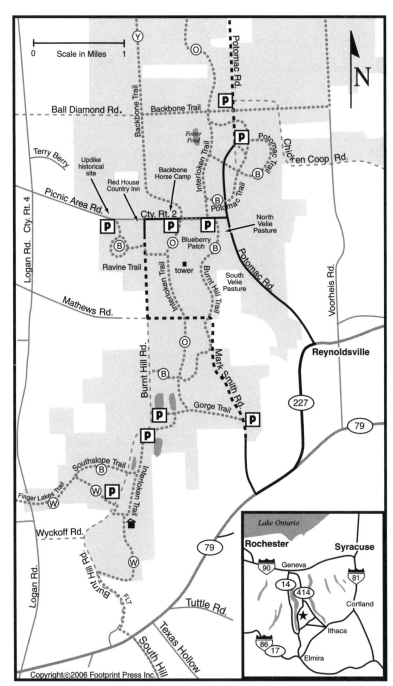

Finger Lakes National Forest (South Section)

64.

Finger Lakes National Forest

Location:	Southeast side of Seneca Lake, Schuyler County
Dogs:	OK on leash
Contact:	Finger Lakes National Forest
	5218 State Route 414, Hector, NY 14841
	(607) 546-4470

Trail	Color	Length	Uses
Ravine	Blue	1.0 mile	Hike
Gorge		1.25 miles	Hike
Interloken	Orange	12 miles	Hike, Ski
Potomac	Blue	2.25 miles	Hike, Ski
Finger Lakes	White	4.0 miles	Hike, Ski
Southslope	Blue	0.75 mile	Hike, Ski
Burnt Hill	Blue	2.5 miles	Hike, Ski, Horse, Snowmobile
Backbone	Yellow	5.5 miles	Hike, Ski, Horse, Snowmobile
No-Tan-Takto	Yellow	4.5 miles	Hike, Ski, Horse, Snowmobile

The Finger Lakes National Forest encompasses 16,000 acres of land and has over 30 miles of interconnecting hiking trails. Hiking during hunting season is not recommended since the national forest is open to hunting.

On foot, you can explore the deep forests and steep hills of this varied countryside. The forest contains a five-acre blueberry patch. What better treat on any excursion than devouring a handful of freshly picked blueberries? July and August are the best months to find ripe blueberries. This forest also offers overnight camping and a privately owned bed-and-breakfast (Red House Country Inn B&B) nearby, making it a perfect weekend getaway. The Blueberry Patch Campground within the National Forest charges a fee on a first come, first served basis. Free camping is also allowed throughout the National Forest. Contact the Finger Lakes National Forest for additional information on camping.

The Iroquois Indians originally inhabited the area around the Finger Lakes National Forest. In 1790 the area was divided into 600-acre military lots and distributed among Revolutionary War veterans as payment for their services. These early settlers cleared the land for production of hay and small grains such as buckwheat. As New York City grew, a strong

The path winds below an apple tree — break time anyone?

market for these products developed, encouraging more intensive agriculture. The farmers prospered until the middle of the nineteenth century, when a series of events occurred. These included the popularity of motorized transportation in urban centers (reducing the number of horses to be fed), gradual depletion of the soil resource, and competition from midwestern agriculture due to the opening of the Erie Canal.

Between 1890 and the Great Depression, over a million acres of farmland were abandoned in south central New York State. In the 1930s it was obvious that farmers in many parts of the country could no longer make a living from their exhausted land. Environmental damage worsened as they cultivated the land more and more intensively to make ends meet. Several pieces of legislation were passed, including the Emergency Relief Act of 1933 and the Bankhead-Jones Farm Tenant Act of 1937, to address these problems. A new government agency, the Resettlement Administration, was formed to carry out the new laws. This agency not only directed the relocation of farmers to better land or other jobs, but also coordinated the purchase of marginal farmland by the federal government.

Between 1938 and 1941, over 100 farms were purchased in the Finger Lakes National Forest area and administered by the Soil Conservation Service. Because this was done on a willing-seller, willing-buyer basis, the resulting federal ownership resembled a patchwork quilt. The land was named the Hector Land Use Area and was planted with conifers and turned into grazing fields to stabilize the soil. Individual livestock owners were allowed to graze animals on the pasture land to show how less intensive agriculture could still make productive use of the land.

By the 1950s many of the objectives of the Hector Land Use Area had been met, and the public was becoming interested in the concept of multiple uses of public land. In 1954 administration responsibilities were transferred to the U.S. Forest Service. The name was changed to the Hector Ranger District, Finger Lakes National Forest, in 1985.

Today this National Forest is used for recreation, hunting, forestry, grazing of private livestock, preservation of wildlife habitat, education, and research. It is a treasure available for us all to enjoy.

The Ravine Trail

Directions: From Route 414, head east on County Route 2 (Picnic Area Road). The parking area for the Ravine Trail is on the right, past County Route 4 (Logan Road).
N42º 29.021 - W76º 48.767 (map on page 252)

Alternative Parking: Blueberry Patch Campsite parking lot on Picnic Area Road

Hiking Time: 3 hour loop

Length: 5.7-mile loop (combine with the Gorge Trail Loop for an 11.4-mile loop)

Difficulty: 👣 👣 👣

Surface: Dirt and grass trails

Trail Markings: Excellent signs at junctions, plus blue and orange blazes

Uses:

This loop starts and ends on the Ravine Trail where Tug Hollow Creek dug its way to a bed of flat slate slabs. The biggest climbs are in and out of this ravine. In between it covers flatter portions on the Interloken and Burnt Hill Trails. Most of the trail is in the woods, but a few sections take you through active cow pastures.

Across Picnic Area Road from the parking lot is the Updike Historical Site. A short walk on the trail takes you to the remains of a once prosperous farm, owned by the Updike family for generations. It was originally built by Renselaer and Orvilla Updike in 1852 and passed to their son

Alvah and his wife Harriet in 1902. The stone house foundation and concrete slab from the barn are still visible.

Trail Directions

- Head south on the trail following the blue blazes.
- Bear left at the "loop trail" sign.
- Cross a wooden bridge on this narrow woods trail.
- The ravine begins to form on your right.
- At 0.3 mile, turn left at the "trail" sign.
- Head down steps into the ravine. Pass a trail to the right that will become part of your return loop. Continue straight (SE) and head uphill.
- Bear left at the "trail" sign toward the top of the hill.
- Reach Burnt Hill Road at 0.7 mile.
- Turn right (S) on the road for 25 yards.
- Turn left to continue on Ravine Trail and continue a gradual uphill.
- Reach a "T" at 1.0 mile. Turn left (N) on the orange-blazed Interloken Trail.
- Bear left and stay on the orange-blazed trail. Several small side trails lead to the Blueberry Patch Campsites.
- Continue straight past a clearing and small trails on the right.
- Reach Picnic Area Road at 1.3 miles. Turn right (E) on the road.
- Pass the entrance to Blueberry Patch Campground.
- Pass the junction for Interloken Trail on the left, continuing straight for a short distance on Picnic Area Road.
- At a parking area on the right, turn right toward Burnt Hill Trail.
- Head southeast from the parking area, then turn right (S) at the "trail" sign, walking along the edge of a pasture.

We're visitors to this beautiful hilltop. The cows enjoy it year-round.
256

- The trail bends right then left around the end of the pasture.
- At 1.9 miles follow the "trail" sign back into the woods.
- The trail bends left at the next "trail" sign.
- Continue south through a gate into South Velie pasture. This is an active cow pasture, so be sure to latch the gate behind you.
- Follow the blue blazes on posts through the pasture. Notice a pond to the left and a communication tower to the right.
- Re-enter the woods at 2.4 miles.
- Pass through a second gate, then cross Mathews Road and a parking area. Continue straight (S) through the woods.
- Cross a seasonal stream.
- The trail winds placidly through the woods, gradually downhill.
- At 3.3 miles, reach the intersection of Interloken Trail and turn right (N) onto Interloken Trail (orange-blazed).
  [Turn left here if you want to join the Ravine and Gorge Loop trails.]
- Walk gradually uphill through a green tree tunnel. If it's late summer, watch for ripe berries along the way.
- At 3.8 miles, reach Mathews Road and a parking area. Cross the road.
- Cross through the pasture, following orange blazes on posts. Enjoy the panoramic view of Seneca Lake valley to your left. A big old apple tree in the pasture makes a perfect shaded break spot.
- Pass another gate and return to woods, heading downhill.
- Cross a seasonal creek bed.
- At 4.6 miles, reach Ravine Trail and turn left (W), downhill.
- Reach Burnt Hill Road. Turn right (N) for 25 yards.
- Turn left (W) to continue on the trail.
- Reach a "trail" sign at 5.2 miles. Bear right and head downhill into the gully.
- Cross a seasonal streambed.
- Turn left (SW) at the next trail junction.
- Ford the streambed of Tug Hollow Creek. If the water is low, check for fossils in the flat rocks.
- Climb out of the ravine.
- The ravine will appear on your right, far below.
- Cross a small wooden bridge.
- At 5.6 miles, pass the Ravine Loop Trail junction to the right. Continue straight.
- Reach the parking area on Picnic Area Road.

Date Hiked: _____

Notes:

Gorge Trail Loop

Directions: From Route 414, head east on Mathews Road, then turn south on Burnt Hill Road. The parking area for Gorge Trail is on the left. N42º 27.363 - W76º 48.373

Alternative Parking: Two other parking areas farther south on Burnt Hill Road

Alternative Parking: The parking area on Mark Smith Road N42º 27.292- W76º 47.185

Hiking Time: 2.7 hour loop

Length: 5.4-mile loop (combine with the Ravine Trail Loop for an 11.4-mile loop)

Difficulty: 👟👟👟👟

Surface: Dirt and grass trails

Trail Markings: Excellent signs at junctions, plus orange, white, and blue blazes

Uses: 🚶

This hike is entirely in the woods, shaded by the trees above. You start with a walk into the gorge where Hector Falls Creek carved its way to the slate bedrock. For part of the trek you'll walk a portion of the Finger Lakes Trail which stretches across New York State for 557 miles from Allegany State Park to the Catskill Mountains.

A well-marked entrance to the Interloken Trail.

Trail Directions

- From the Gorge Trail parking area on Burnt Hill Road, head east on the trail.
- Pass a pond on your left.
- Follow the "trail" sign to the left and enter the woods.
- Pass another pond on the left. Reach a trail intersection, and turn left onto Interloken Trail.
- Head downhill and cross a boardwalk.
- Cross a seasonal stream.
- At 0.3 mile, reach the second intersection of Interloken Trail. This time continue straight, uphill on Gorge Trail.
- Cross another seasonal stream.
- Head downhill.
- Cross two more seasonal streams.
- There's a steep downhill into the gorge.
- Pass two "trail" signs.
- Cross a seasonal feeder stream.
- Walk parallel with the rock-strewn streambed. (You can turn around at this point and decrease the loop length by 0.8 mile.)
- Head uphill through a pine woods.
- Walk downhill to the parking area on Mark Smith Road. You've come 1.1 miles.
- Turn around and retrace your steps, heading uphill.
- Pass the gully where water cascades down the slate slabs.
- Cross a seasonal stream and "trail" sign.
- Bear right and head uphill at the second "trail" sign.
- Cross two seasonal streams.
- Head uphill.
- Cross another seasonal stream.
- At 1.6 miles, reach the Interloken Trail junction. Continue straight on Interloken Trail.
- Cross a seasonal stream, then a boardwalk.
- At the next junction (1.7 miles), bear left on the orange-blazed Interloken Trail.
- The vegetation becomes more lush on the forest floor.
- Reach Burnt Hill Road, and continue straight (W).
- Pass a pond on the left.
- Wind around the pond on a grass-covered dike.
- Re-enter the woods.
- Pass through a muddy stretch torn up by horse hooves.

- Reach the junction of Southslope Trail, and continue straight (SW) on Interloken Trail.
- Eventually enter a pine forest where the planted trees all form rows.
- Begin a gradual downhill as grasses line the trail.
- Reach the Finger Lakes Trail intersection at 3.0 miles. Continue straight (W) on the white-blazed FLT. (Down the trail to the left is a shelter.)
- Continue downhill.
- Reach Burnt Hill Road and turn right (NE) following the white blazes.
- The trail turns left (N) into the woods, shortly after a parking area on the left.
- Head downhill.
- Cross a seasonal feeder stream.
- Cross a wooden bridge. (You'll begin to see markers for North Country Trail. This trail will eventually extend across the country and is using portions of the Finger Lakes Trail through New York State.)
- A gradual downhill, then cross a small wooden bridge.
- At 3.7 miles, turn right (N) on Southslope Trail, following the blue blazes.
- Emerge from the woods, and cross through a scrub field.
- Return to the woods.
- Cross a seasonal stream, then a boardwalk.
- Cross two small culverts.
- Cross Burnt Hill Road.
- Bear right (E) at the pond.
- Cross the end of the pond on stones, and continue on the blue trail.
- Follow the blue blazes through the woods and gradually uphill.
- Reach a "T" at 4.5 miles, and turn left (NE) on the orange-blazed Interloken Trail.
- Pass through a muddy stretch torn up by horse hooves.
- Reach a pond and follow the grass-covered dike around it.
- Continue straight past two parking areas off Burnt Hill Road.
- Pass the Interloken Trail sign.
- At the next junction, turn left (W) on Gorge Trail. You've come 5.2 miles.
- Pass the pond on the right.
- Bear right at the "trail" sign on the grass dike around the pond.
- Reach the parking area.

Date Hiked: _____

Notes:

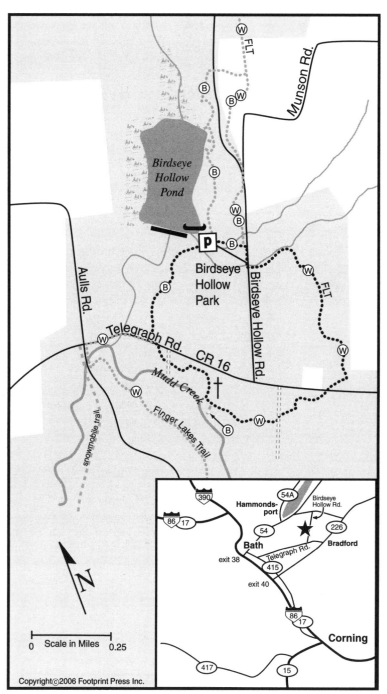

Birdseye Hollow State Forest

65.

Birdseye Hollow State Forest

Location:	Southeast of Keuka Lake, Steuben County
Directions:	From Bath, follow Route 415 south, then County Route 16 (Telegraph Road) east. Turn left (N) onto Birdseye Hollow Road. Birdseye Hollow County Park will be 0.4 mile north, on the left. N42° 22.214- W76° 8.898
Hiking Time:	1.0 hour loop
Length:	2.0-mile loop
Difficulty:	👣 👣
Surface:	Dirt trails
Trail Markings:	White and blue blazes
Uses:	🚶
Dogs:	OK on leash
Contact:	Finger Lakes Trail Conference
	6111 Visitor Center Road, Mt. Morris, NY 14510
	(585) 658-9320 www.fingerlakestrail.org
	N.Y.S. Department of Environmental Conservation
	7291 Coon Road, Bath, NY 14810-9728
	(607) 776-2165 www.dec.state.ny.us

Birdseye Hollow County Park offers picnic tables, grills, a pavilion, playground, and outhouses. It also has a boardwalk to an observation deck in the pond, a favorite place of people fishing and birdwatching. The hike described is an easy ramble through the woods on a section of the Finger Lakes Trail. If you like exploring old graveyards, you're in luck. You'll pass one in the woods, with grave markers dating to the early 1800s. The return leg on the blue-blazed trail can be wet in spring and after rain storms.

Trail Description
•From the parking area, walk back up the entrance road along the left side. You'll begin to see blue blazes.
•At a green and white "Trail" sign, the trail enters the woods, heading southeast.

A long deck winds into the Birdseye Hollow Pond.

- Soon continue straight as the trail turns to white blazes. (Pass a white-blazed trail to the left. This is the Finger Lakes Trail, heading north.)
- Reach Birdseye Hollow Road, and turn right (S) along the road.
- Shortly after the park entrance, turn left (E) to cross Birdseye Hollow Road and enter the woods.
- The trail will parallel a creek bed.
- Follow the white blazes as they twist and turn through a young forest.
- At 0.8 mile, reach a dirt road near some mobile homes, but bear left to continue in the woods.
- Quickly reach County Route 16. Turn right (W) and follow the road for a short distance, then turn left back into the woods.
- Cross an old logging road, still following the white blazes.
- Continue straight (N) past a blue trail junction. (The blue trail is a low water shortcut across a creek for people following the Finger Lakes Trail.)
- Pass the old cemetery on the right.
- At 1.4 miles, pass a cellar hole from an old farmhouse, then cross a logging road.
- Reach County Route 16 at 1.5 miles, and turn left (NW) following the road.
- In about 25 yards, watch carefully for the blue trail blazes on the other side of the road (NE) and head into the woods before reaching the bridge.
- Emerge to a grass area in the park, and follow the edge of the pond back to the parking area.

Date Hiked: _____

Notes:

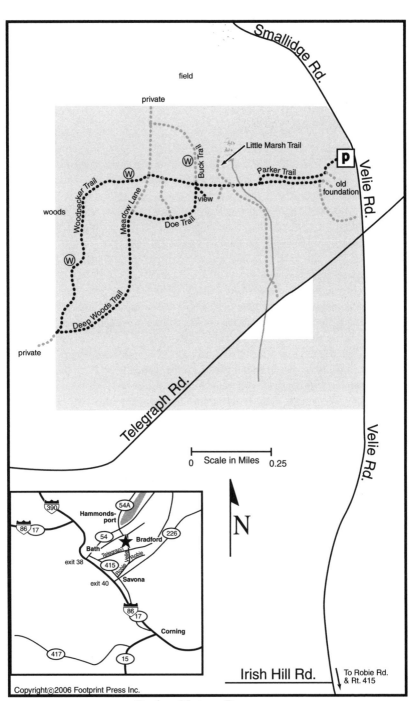

Parker Nature Preserve

66.

Parker Nature Preserve

Location:	Bath, Steuben County
Directions:	From I-86 take exit 40 in Savona, take Route 226 into Savona. Turn left onto Route 415, then right onto Robie Road. Turn left onto Velie Road. Pass Irish Hill and Telegraph Roads, then park on the left in the grass parking area. N42o 20.449 - W77o 11.846
Hiking Time:	45 minute loop
Length:	1.5-mile loop (darkened trails)
	2.2 miles total trails
Difficulty:	👢 👢 👢
Surface:	Mowed-grass and woods trails
Trail Markings:	Some white blazes
Uses:	🚶
Dogs:	OK on leash
Contact:	Finger Lakes Land Trust
	202 East Court Street, Ithaca, NY 14850
	(607) 275-9487 www.fllt.org

Parker Nature Preserve consists of 170 acres of varied terrain. It begins from the parking area on Velie Road in grasslands and climbs a hill through young forest to a high meadow then into a mature forest on top of the hill. This land was donated by Gene and Joan Lane. Bring your binoculars. The varied habitats are great for birdwatching.

Trail Directions
•From the parking area, head uphill on the mowed-grass trail. It doesn't matter which track you take as long as you head uphill.
•Continue uphill as the grass track gets steeper then eventually turns into a white-blazed woods trail. Pass several trails to the left and right along the way.
•Follow the white-blazed Woodpecker Trail as it bends left through a mature forest, then turn left onto the Deep Woods Trail.
•The trail will return to mowed grass. Take the next right to head downhill on Doe Trail.

A valley view from Parker Nature Preserve.

•A short trail to the right leads to a clearing with a view.
•When Doe Trail intersects with the main trail, turn right and continue downhill to the parking area.

Date Hiked: _____

Notes:

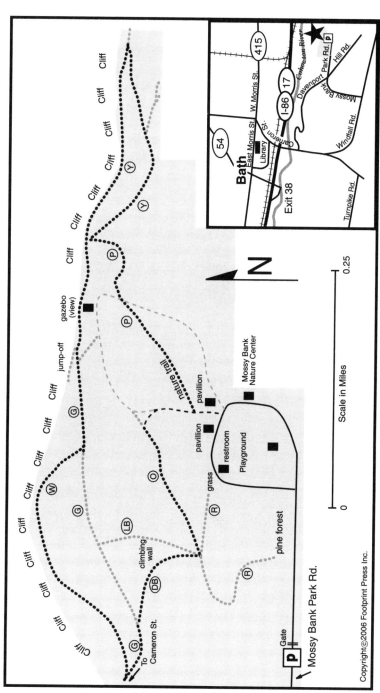

Mossy Bank Park

67.

Mossy Bank Park

Location:	Bath, Steuben County
Directions:	From Route 17 (I-86) take exit 38 to Route 54 N. Turn right onto E. Morris Street, then bear right at the "Y" following a sign for bike route 17. Pass the library on the right, then turn right just before Fagan's Furniture onto Cameron Street. Continue west across the railroad tracks, under I-86, and over the Cohocton River. Follow the green and white signs to Mossy Bank Park, and park before the gates (Oct. 16 - April 30) or along the loop within the park. N42º 19.174 - W77º 19.275
Hiking Time:	1 hour loop
Length:	1.8-mile loop (darkened trail)
	2.3 miles of trails
Difficulty:	👣 👣
Surface:	Woods trails
Trail Markings:	Colored blazes
Uses:	🚶 🚶
Dogs:	OK
Contact:	Village of Bath, NY
	PO Box 668, 110 Liberty Street, Bath, NY 14810
	(607) 776-3811

Some say this park offers the "best views in western New York." It's hard to dispute this claim as you stand on the edge of a cliff overlooking Bath and the Cohocton River valley. Even without the panoramic view, this place would be special. The trails cross through hemlock forests and are easy-to-follow. Most are on the upland portion of the park and are fairly flat. Some head downhill a bit to the lowland section, perched above the cliff. These have a some hills.

The Mossy Bank Nature Center is a log cabin classroom used by nature groups and schools for the study of natural resources.

Mossy Bank overlooks the Cohocton River valley.

Trail	Distance	Trail	Distance
Red Trail	0.3 mile	Green Trail	0.5 mile
Orange Trail	0.2 mile	White Trail	0.3 mile
Light Blue Trail	0.1 mile	Purple Nature Trail	0.2 mile
Dark Blue Trail	0.1 mile	Yellow Trail	0.5-mile loop

Trail Directions
- From the paved loop in the park, follow the gravel trail between the two pavilions.
- Turn right to follow the purple-blazed nature trail.
- When it ends, turn right onto the yellow trail.
- Follow the yellow loop, continuing back along the cliff edge.
- Continue straight, past the gazebo, onto the green trail.
- Turn right onto the white trail.
- At it's end, turn left onto the green trail.
- Turn right onto the dark blue trail.
- At the end, turn left onto the orange trail, then bear right onto the the gravel trail that leads back to the paved park loop.

Date Hiked: _____

Notes:

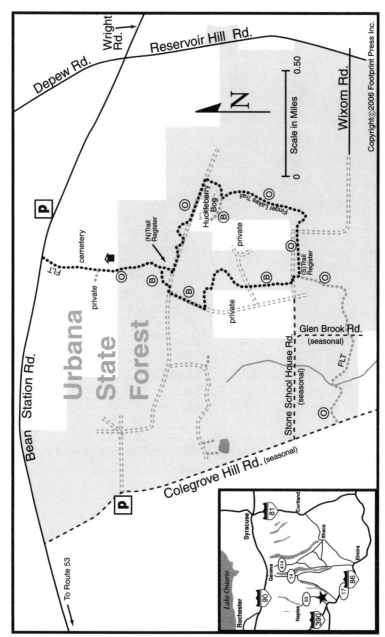

Urbana State Forest

68.

Urbana State Forest

Location:	Between Prattsburgh and Hammondsport, Steuben County
Directions:	From the south end of Canandaigua Lake, take Route 53 south. South of Prattsburgh, turn east on Bean Station Road. Pass Dineharts Crossing Road, then Colegrove Hill Road, both on the right. Watch for signs for the Finger Lakes Trail (FLT) on both sides of Bean Station Road (also called Swamp Road). The parking area is along Bean Station Road, just east of the trail crossing. N42° 28.660 - W77° 14.428
Alternative Parking:	A dirt pull-off parking area along Colegrove Hill Road. N42° 28.320 - W77° 16.000
Hiking Time:	2.3 hour loop
Length:	4.8-mile loop
Difficulty:	👣 👣 👣
Surface:	Dirt trails
Trail Markings:	Orange and blue blazes
Uses:	🚶 🎿
Dogs:	OK
Contact:	Finger Lakes Trail Conference 6111 Visitor Center Road, Mt. Morris, NY 14510 (585) 658-9320 www.fingerlakestrail.org
	N.Y.S. Department of Environmental Conservation 7291 Coon Road, Bath, NY 14810-9728 (607) 776-2165 ext. 10 www.dec.state.ny.us

Urbana State Forest sits on a plateau west of Keuka Lake. Your initial challenge will be to climb to the plateau. Once there, the hike is fairly level. In the 1800s this area was farmland. You'll walk some abandoned country lanes with larger roadside trees, plentiful apple trees, and rocks cleared from fields.

This trail has a special treat. It leads you around Huckleberry Bog, a rare occurrence at such a high elevation. Bogs such as this one began their life

Begin this hike
with a bit of rural humor.

as glaciers retreated from the area. They left depressions, called glacial ponds, which filled with water from melting snow or rain. With no inlet or outflow of fresh water, the ponds then relied on rainwater for replenishment. Due to the low mineral content of melted ice and rainwater, these ponds were not attractive to the usual microscopic flora such as bacteria and fungi. Instead, the ponds were colonized by sphagnum mosses and heaths such as leatherleaf. The sphagnum moss consumed what minerals existed and excreted acids, producing acidic water. Over long periods of time, the moss built layers upon itself. The compressed moss formed a quaking mat over the water and became peat.

In a mature bog, the moss may cover almost all the water and become so thick that it can even support a person's weight. Walking on a bog is like walking on a wet sponge.

Because the bog pond is replenished only by rainwater, it is low in oxygen. Add this to the low mineral content and acidity and you have a unique environment, one that is not enticing to most wildlife and one that supports rare species of plants. Bogs are home to carnivorous plants that trap and eat insects. These include the pitcher plant, sundew, and butterwort. They are also home to flowering orchids, water willow (a loosestrife), leatherleaf (an evergreen in the heath family), and wild cranberry plants. Most trees dislike the acidic conditions of the bog. The exception is the tamarack or larch, which can often be found along the edges of a bog.

The peat from bogs was a precious commodity in years gone by. For centuries, northern Europeans dried the peat and burned it as fuel. It has twice the heating value of wood and two-thirds the heating value of coal. In World War I peat was used to wrap wounds because of its anti-bacterial properties and absorbency. It has also been used as diapers. Today people add sphagnum moss (peat) to soil for potting houseplants and landscape gardening because of its water retention properties.

The hugging trees in Urbana State Forest.

Huckleberry Bog supports high bush and low bush blueberries, and sphagnum moss, but no huckleberries. Huckleberry Bog is a misnomer that got applied to this area and stuck. High bush blueberries are the 4 to 5 foot tall bushes that surround the observation deck overlooking the bog. Their berries are small but tasty. The less than one-foot tall bushes that carpet the forest, especially along the blue trail, are low bush blueberries. These berries are tasty too, but even smaller.

Another rare treat is the Nature Trail Guide, which was produced by trail maintainer Irene Szabo and Robert Hughes' science class at Wayland-

Follow the painted blazes.

Cohocton High School. This 32-page booklet can be picked up at two locations along the trail. It describes the trees, plants, and farm remnants found along the way. Your walk can become a free nature study and a full day adventure, thanks to Irene's great efforts. Please return the guide after use, so it will be available for the next nature lover.

As part of the Bristol Hills Branch of the Finger Lakes Trail, this trail is well blazed. You'll follow orange blazes for the first half and blue blazes for

274

most of the return. (Branch trails off the main white-blazed Finger Lakes Trail are blazed orange.) The trail will wind on and off the country lanes and forest paths, so follow the blazes carefully.

Camping is allowed in Urbana State Forest. For stays of three days or longer, or by groups of 10 or more, obtain a free camping permit from the D.E.C. Regional Ranger at the address above.

A longer hike (a little over 7-miles long) is possible using the Finger Lakes Trail south of the described hike, a segment of dirt Colegrove Hill Road and the old double-track road that leads east from the parking area on Colegrove Hill Road.

Trail Directions
•From the parking area along Bean Station Road, cross the road and head west along the road to the FLT (Finger Lakes Trail) crossing.
•At the yellow FLT signs, turn left, crossing a small wooden bridge, onto the trail. Begin following orange blazes.
•Pass Covell Cemetery, and continue uphill following the blazes.
•Pass Evangeline shelter (with an outhouse). N42º 28.469 - W77º 14.566
•At 0.7 mile, reach the junction with the blue trail. (This will be your return loop.) Continue straight following orange blazes.
•Pass the north trail register at N42º 28.085 - W77º 14.589.
•The trail will wind on and off an old woods lane. Follow the orange blazes carefully.
•At 1.4 miles the orange trail turns right (S).
•Pass a small deck overlooking the bog.
•At 1.6 miles a blue spur trail (0.15-mile long) will be on the right. (It leads part way around the bog.) Bear left staying on the orange-blazed trail.
•Cross a country lane.
•At 2.6 miles, cross a stream, then reach the south trail register (N42º 27.472 - W77º 14.606), and turn right onto the blue-blazed trail.
•Shortly jog left on an old road, then right onto a trail, still following blue blazes.
•Pass a dirt lane that leads to private property.
•At 2.9 miles, turn right onto an old road.
•At 3.5 miles, an unblazed lane heads off to the left and the blue trail bends right. (This lane leads to the parking area on Colegrove Hill Road).
•At 4.0 miles, reach the orange-blazed trail intersection, and turn left.
•Follow the orange blazes downhill to Bean Station Road.

Date Hiked: _____
Notes:

Definitions

Aqueduct: A stone, wood, or cement trough built to carry water over an existing creek or river. The world's largest aqueduct for its time was built in Rochester to span the Genesee River. Eleven stone arches were erected, spanning 804 feet, to withstand the annual floods of this wild river.

Arboretum: A tree garden where a variety of trees are planted and labeled for study and enjoyment.

Bog: An acid-rich, wet, poorly drained, spongy area characterized by plants such as sedges, heaths, and sphagnum.

Corduroy: A method of spanning a wet section of trail by laying logs perpendicular to the trail. This creates a bumpy effect like corduroy material.

Deciduous: Describes trees that lose their leaves in winter.

Dike: An earthen bank constructed to hold water.

Drumlin: An elongated or oval hill created from glacial debris.

Eft: A newt or small, usually bright-colored, semiaquatic salamander in its terrestrial stage of development.

Esker: A ridge of debris formed when a river flowed under a glacier in an icy tunnel. Rocky material accumulated on the tunnel beds, and when the glacier melted, a ridge of rubble remained.

Feeder: A diverted stream, brook, or other water source used to maintain water level in a canal.

Fulling mill: A mill for cleaning wool and producing cloth.

GPS: Global Positioning System; using satellites to triangulate your position on earth.

Gristmill: A mill for grinding grain into flour.

Headrace: A trough or tunnel for conveying water to a point of industrial application.

Herbaceous: A seed-producing plant that does not develop persistent woody tissue, but dies down at the end of a growing season.

Impoundments: Areas of marshland and ponds created by man-made earthen dikes.

Jewelweed: Also called touch-me-not, this plant is a member of the impatiens family. It grows in moist areas with a translucent stem and small snapdragon-like flowers in yellow, orange, or pink. The leaves shine silvery under water, hence the name jewelweed. The crushed plant has historically been used as a treatment for poison ivy, but recent studies show that it's not effective.

Leatherleaf: A shrub that produces white, bell-like flowers in spring and grows on top of sphagnum moss,allowing other plants to gain a foothold.

Marsh: An area of soft, wet land.

Mule: The sterile offspring of a male donkey and a female horse. Mules were often used to pull boats along the Erie Canal.

Purple loosestrife: An aggressive perennial imported from Europe, these blazing magenta flowering plants are spreading across American wetlands and crowding out native plants. The name derives from the early practice of placing this plant over the yoke of quarrelsome oxen. The plant was said to help the oxen "loose their strife" or quiet down.

Rebar: Round metal bars used to give structural strength (reinforce ment) to cement.

Riparian zone: Land located on the bank of a natural waterway.

Sawmill: A mill for cutting trees into lumber.

Snag: Standing dead trees which provide dens and cavities for wildlife.

Sphagnum moss: A type of moss that grows in bogs and has an incredible capacity to hold water. It's estimated that this moss can can soak up over 100 times its own weight in water. In bogs where acids build up and oxygen is lacking, the moss compresses rather than degrades, and forms peat. Dried, shredded, and packed in bales, sphagnum moss is sold as peat moss and used by gardeners to retain moisture in soil.

Swamp: Wet, spongy land saturated and sometimes partially or intermittently covered with water.

Switchbacks: Winding the trail back and forth across the face of a steep area to make the incline more gradual.

Waste weir: A dam along the side of the canal which allows overflow water to dissipate into a side waterway.

Wide water: An area on a canal where the water is unusually wide, so that boats can easily turn around.

Trails Under 2 Miles

Trails 2 to 4 Miles

Trails Over 4 Miles

Contains a Wheelchair Accessible Trail

(For many more wheelchair accessible trails see the guidebook: *Take Your Bike - Family Rides in New York's Finger Lakes Region*.)

1 Boot Trails

2 Boot Trails

3 Boot Trails

4 Boot Trails

4 Boot Trails

Trails to Waterfalls

Trails to Scenic Views

Other Special Trails

Word Index

Other Books Available from Footprint Press, Inc.

Cross-country Skiing and Snowshoeing:

Snow Trails – Cross-country Ski and Snowshoe in Central and Western NY
ISBN# 0-9656974-52   U.S. $16.95
80 mapped locations for winter fun on skis or snowshoes.

Hiking:

200 Waterfalls in Central & Western New York - A Finders' Guide
ISBN#1-930480-01-6   U.S. $18.95
Discover over 200 wondrous waterfalls.

Peak Experiences – Hiking the Highest Summits in NY, County by County
ISBN# 0-9656974-01   U.S. $16.95
A guide to the highest point in each county of New York
State.

Take A Hike! Family Walks in the Rochester Area
ISBN# 0-9656974-79   U.S. $16.95
60 day hikes within a 15-mile radius of Rochester, N.Y.

Take A Hike! Family Walks in the Finger Lakes & Genesee Valley Region
ISBN# 0-9656974-95   U.S. $16.95
51 day hike trails throughout central and western New York.

Bruce Trail – An Adventure Along the Niagara Escarpment
ISBN# 0-9656974-36   U.S. $16.95
Learn the secrets of long-distance backpackers on a five-week
hike in Ontario, Canada, as they explore the abandoned
Welland Canal routes, caves, ancient cedar forests, and white
cobblestone beaches along Georgian Bay.

Backpacking Trails of Central & Western New York State
ISBN# none   U.S. $2.00
A 10-page booklet describing the backpackable trails of
central and western NYS with contact information to obtain
maps and trail guides.

Bird Watching:

*Birding in Central & Western New York – Best Trails &
Water Routes for Finding Birds*
ISBN# 1-930480-00-8   U.S. $16.95
70 of the best places to spot birds on foot, from a car,
or from a canoe.

Bicycling:

Take Your Bike! Family Rides in the Rochester Area
ISBN# 1-930480-02-4   U.S. $18.95

Converted railroad beds, paved bike paths and woods trails, combine to create the 42 safe bicycle adventures within an easy drive of Rochester, N.Y.

Take Your Bike! Family Rides in the Finger Lakes & Genesee Valley Region
ISBN# 0-9656974-44   U.S. $16.95
Converted railroad beds, woods trails, and little-used country roads combine to create the 40 safe bicycle adventures through central and western New York State.

Take Your Bike! Family Rides in New York's Finger Lakes Region
ISBN# 1-930480-22-9   U.S. $19.95
2nd edition - 43 bike trails in the Finger Lakes Region.

Explore History:

Cobblestone Quest - Road Tours of New York's Historic Buildings
ISBN# 1-930480-19-9   U.S. $19.95
17 self-guided tours for observing the history and diversity of unique cobblestone buildings that are found within a 65-mile radius of Rochester, NY, and nowhere else. Enjoy the tours by car, motorcycle, or bicycle.

Canoeing & Kayaking:

Take a Paddle - Western New York Quiet Water for Canoes & Kayaks
ISBN# 1-930480-23-7   U.S. $18.95
Offering over 250 miles of flat-water creeks and rivers, and 20 ponds and lakes, this guide provides a fun way to explore Western New York.

Take a Paddle - Finger Lakes New York Quiet Water for Canoes & Kayaks
ISBN# 1-930480-24-5   U.S. $18.95
Offering over 370 miles of flat-water creeks and rivers, and 35 ponds and lakes, this guide provides a fun way to explore the beautiful Finger Lakes region.

Self-help:

Alter – A Simple Path to Emotional Wellness
ISBN# 0-9656974-87   U.S. $16.95
A self-help manual that assists in recognizing and changing emotional blocks and limiting belief systems, using easy-to-learn techniques of biofeedback to retrieve subliminal information and achieve personal transformation.

For sample maps and chapters explore web site:
www.footprintpress.com

Yes, I'd like to order Footprint Press books:

#

____	*Take A Hike! Family Walks in NY's Finger Lakes*	$19.95
____	*Take Your Bike! Family Rides in NY's Finger Lakes*	$19.95
____	*200 Waterfalls in Central & Western NY*	$18.95
____	*Take a Paddle - Western NY*	$18.95
____	*Take a Paddle - Finger Lakes NY*	$18.95
____	*Cobblestone Quest*	$19.95
____	*Peak Experiences—Hiking the Highest Summits of NY*	$16.95
____	*NYS County Summit Club patch*	$2.00
____	*Snow Trails—Cross-country Ski & Snowshoe*	$16.95
____	*Birdng in Central & Western NY*	$16.95
____	*Take A Hike! Family Walks in the Rochester Area*	$16.95
____	*Take A Hike! Family Walks in the Finger Lakes & Genesee Valley*	$16.95
____	*Take Your Bike! Family Rides in the Rochester Area*	$18.95
____	*Take Your Bike! Family Rides in the Finger Lakes & Genesee Valley*	$16.95
____	*Bruce Trail—Adventure Along the Niagara Escarpment*	$16.95
____	*Backpacking Trails of Central & Western NYS*	$2.00
____	*Alter—A Simple Path to Emotional Wellness*	$16.95

Sub-total:	$_____
FL State and Canadian residents add 7% tax:	$_____
Shipping & handling:	$ 3.00
Total enclosed:	$_____

Your Name: _____

Address: _____

City: _____ State (Province): _____

Zip (Postal Code): _____ Country: _____

Make check payable and mail to:
Footprint Press, Inc.
303 Pine Glen Court, Englewood, FL 34223

Or order through web site: **www.footprintpress.com**